'Laurie Mellor is an observer ⌐
historical knowledge and res⌐
prophets in our recent past an⌐
can use anyone to make a differ⌐⌐⌐, wiiuiever their circumstances.
I really enjoyed this book.'

John Noble, speaker & author, formerly Chair of the National
Charismatic Leaders Conference for 24 years

'This is a great read. I couldn't put it down!

'Laurie Mellor has written an excellent, concise history of the
English, exploring the complex fabric of what has made Britain
"Great". Whilst giving no easy answers, this book convincingly
points us forward to engage with the issues; change always
belongs to the passionate minority.'

Richard Hubbard, CEO Links International

'This book will challenge you, tread on your toes, and invoke all
kinds of emotional response in you but to remain passive and
passionless is not an option. The challenge to make a difference
both as individuals and church must be taken seriously if we are
to see an answer to the prayer Your Kingdom come.'

Rodney Kingstone, author & speaker

'Laurie's research is far reaching and he dares to ask questions
many only think about; this is a thought provoking read.'

Norman Barnes
Founder Links International, speaker and author

Also by Laurie Mellor

A Desert Song

Sales Success in Tough Times

The Sick Rose

England's Spiritual Crisis

Laurie Mellor

DREAM
DEPOT

Special discounts on bulk copies of this book are available: for details please contact the Publishers

Dream Depot Ltd.
P.O. Box No. 3357, Littlehampton, West Sussex, BN16 9GJ
Tel: +44 (0)1903 882007
Fax: +44 (0)1903 882004
E-mail: office@dreamdepot.co.uk

First Published in Great Britain, October 2010
by Dream Depot Ltd.

ISBN 978-0-9545979-1-7

Cover design, photography and text designed and produced by Rob Newey, Basic Print & Web
www.basicprintandweb.com

Printed by Verité CM Ltd
www.veritecm.com

DREAM
DEPOT

O Rose, thou art sick
The invisible worm
That flies in the night
In the howling storm
Has found out thy bed of crimson joy;
And his dark secret love
Does thy life destroy.

William Blake
The Sick Rose

For Brenda, Sam & Jamie
and Rich, the Church's own Del Boy

Contents

PART 3 England Present

Preface

I have not attempted a comprehensive history of England over the last two hundred and fifty years, but rather have picked out events and people I believe to be significant in the scheme of things.

I have tried to convey a sense of sadness, of loss, that something beautiful has perished; of a rose trampled on the ground. Tracing the decline of a nation is a difficult, painful exercise and I hope that others will be touched by the same feelings: not just so that we can lose ourselves in an orgy of nostalgia, but so that we can look to the future and fashion new paths made out of old stones.

I acknowledge, with grateful thanks, helpful input and support from John Noble, Sam Mellor, Rob and Elaine Newey and Chris Staight; Rich Hubbard, greatly missed, who opened doors to a new world for me.

Thanks, as always, to my current wife Brenda for her forbearance, helpful comments and constant support.

Laurie Mellor

West Sussex
October 2010

Part 1

The Sick Rose

Chapter 1

The Sick Rose

'England is a land of faith, dreams and melancholy'
Peter Ackroyd

If there is consensus on anything in our country, it must be on twin topics: the weather and the state of the nation. The weather is lousy and the country has gone to the dogs.

There are some obvious lines of enquiry…. in no particular order, credit crunch, dishonest politicians, Europe, USA, foreigners, immigration, loss of Empire, erosion of moral standards, political correctness, a poisonous media, decline of royal family, decline of religion, foreigners again, football hooligans….. the list goes on. Although we shall touch on some of these topics, they are, in the main, effects rather than causes, symptoms rather than diagnoses.

We know that there is something wrong with England, but putting our finger on exactly what is not so easy. Jeremy Paxman: *'The belief that something has rotted in England is widely held: a people cannot spend decades being told their civilisation is in decline and not be affected by it.'* Listen to any group of English people at a party and you will learn what they don't believe: you will be hard pressed, however, to find out what they do believe. Cynicism is corrosive and catching. Our moral and spiritual identity as a nation has been eroded, rubbed away by years of rationalism.

Safe in Taxis

We are now characterised by what we have lost and have no clear identity. Paxman again:

> *Not so long ago everyone knew who the English were. They were polite, unexcitable, reserved, and had hot-water bottles instead of a sex life. As the dominant culture in a*

country which dominated an Empire which dominated the world, they had little need to examine themselves and ask who they were. But something has happened. A new self-confidence seems to have taken hold in Wales and Scotland, while everyone tries to forge a new relationship with Europe, the Irish with notable success. The English are being forced to ask what it is that makes them who they are. The Bulldog Breed ('fearless and philistine, safe in taxis and invaluable in shipwrecks') has no place any longer.

There is a strong case for agreeing with Churchill that the Second World War was England's 'finest hour'. It was England, not Scotland or Ireland or Wales that was most immediately threatened and whose people were most closely involved in the deprivations and threat of the conflict. Maybe this is a major reason for the English confidence in their identity at that time, as opposed to the wider British populace. The Times, in a recent leader, says *'the country has still to fill the void where God used to preside, before organised religion fell away to the point where only 4 per cent go to church regularly.'*

Penny Junor, in her critique of post Thatcher England, puts it thus:

Society has changed out of all recognition in the last sixty years. The values that once underpinned our lives have shifted. Hierarchy and deference have largely gone, and so has respect. We stick two fingers up to authority; we think traditional institutions like Parliament, the Police, the BBC and the Church of England are sleazy and corrupt; we swear, blaspheme and trample all over people, their property and their sensibilities.

The Second World War and its immediate aftermath are the last time in living memory that the English had a positive and clear sense of themselves. In Noel Coward's patriotic film *In Which We Serve*, a fictionalised story of the sinking of HMS Kelly, the survivors of the ship lie in their life-raft recalling the ship's history. What they are really describing is a picture of the strength of England. It is an ordered, hierarchical sort of place where children go dutifully and quietly to bed and the womenfolk know their place. *'Don't make a fuss,'* say the wives to one another, *'we'll have a cup of tea in a minute.' In Which We Serve* was unashamed propaganda for a nation facing the possible destruction of their culture: it shows us how we like to think of ourselves. The picture that emerges - from this and similar films - is of a homely, quiet, dignified, kindly, honourable people who would sooner be tending their gardens than defending the world against a fascist tyranny.

Fingernails Removed

We are superb as a nation at hand-wringing and have made self-criticism into an art form; we overlook all that is good about our society. We are tolerant, moderate, cautious, kind and fair; our country is full of beauty, in our landscape, buildings and heritage. We need to be proud of our country - patriotic, yes - but without the repulsive nationalism of the British National Party. It is reassuring that we can still shout at our Prime Minister without having our fingernails removed.

Moral decay has many manifestations and although in England football violence has decreased, the symbol of the English football fan abroad is the skinhead with ashtray eyes and disposable clothing, screaming obscenities at bewildered football fans around the world. His first cousin can be encountered in Ibiza and various Greek islands, thinking it amusing to get completely wasted, rampaging through bars and night-clubs, hurling insults at anyone who doesn't have English as a first language. His second cousin is alive and well and can be seen in thousands of Indian restaurants across the land, shouting *'over here, Mahatma'* at long-suffering waiters.

I don't want to suggest that morality is all one way traffic and that the Victorian age was blameless in this respect. The issue of young boys being forced up chimneys in the 19th century was a moral one and Victorians largely turned a blind eye. Greed was at the root of it and it needed the patient lobbying of the good Earl Ashley, Lord Shaftesbury, for the practice to be outlawed. We have become less cruel as a nation, both to humans and animals.

There'll always be an Englishman

> *For he might have been a Roosian,*
> *A French, or Turk, or Proosian,*
> *Or perhaps Ital-lian!*
> *But in spite of all temptations*
> *To belong to other nations*
> *He remains an Englishman!*

> Sir William Schwenck Gilbert (1836-1911)
> *HMS Pinafore.*

'Ask any man what nationality he would prefer to be, and ninety nine out of a hundred will tell you that they would prefer to be Englishmen' - Cecil Rhodes. Although the sense of superiority is both staggering and nauseating to our 21st century thinking, such was the incredible self-confidence of the English in Victorian times that pronouncements such as Rhodes' were not unusual.

Sleepwalking

England is sick. The English are sleep-walking into an uncertain future, sedated by consumerism, affluence, political correctness, and indifference. Overcome by materialism, we are aware of enemies hovering on the horizon, but are too passive and apathetic to stir ourselves into action. Militant Islam is clearly a threat. However, the media are doing exactly the same with Islam as they did with the Russians and the Cold War in the sixties – the hysteria being generated is likely to build into a completely unreal paranoia.

Winston Churchill said *'the nation that forgets its past has no future.'* Many in England find it difficult to envisage what the next fifty years holds, because we have become disengaged with our past. Church leader David Pawson predicts that we will be an Islamic state with Shariah law within fifty years. What is needed is re-engagement with our past - not to wallow in the limelight of nostalgia - as a compass for the future. As poet Mike Starkey puts it *'making of old stones, new paths.'*

Hamlet

Societies as well as individuals can be Prince Hamlets, immobilising themselves by self-questioning about the inconsistencies in their character. By contrast, the Victorians were thick-skinned, breezy, not prone to much hesitation or doubt. It is no surprise that Queen Victoria detested Hamlet. A. N. Wilson says of modern day England:

> *We who live in a fragmented society have become like an individual addicted to psychoanalysis, struggling with our uncertainties, picking at our virtues and vices as if they*

were scabs. The Victorian capacity not to do this, to live,
very often, with double standards, is what makes many of
them seem to be humbugs and hypocrites.

God weeps over our re-cycled rectories and chapels which
quietly remind us of a past where He and his people were
in a closer relationship. Now rectories in Herefordshire are
sold to wealthy city types, trying desperately to find some
'rooted-ness', to quote novelist Joanna Trollope. Gothic
chapels in Worthing morph into wine bars and ornate,
disused churches are re-developed as fitness clubs in
Nottingham. Travelling around England can be a sad affair:
every hamlet, village, town and city is overlooked by the
familiar church or chapel, silent, empty witnesses to a
community slowly decaying at the roots.

R. S. Thomas, in his *The Country Clergy*, puts it thus:

Venerable men, their black cloth a little dusty
They left no books
Memorial to their lonely thought
In grey parishes; rather they wrote
On men's hearts and in the minds of young children
Sublime words too soon forgotten.
God in his time
Or out of time will correct this.

This sense of loss is very strong. The diarist and gardener Sir
Roy Strong: *'families are falling apart, religion is discredited. So*
where does our sense of identity come from? What holds this
country together? Not bloody much!' The English are a people
marching backwards into the future; because the Empire is
a distant memory, we are no longer certain who we are. The
resurgence in popularity over the last ten years or so of the
cross of St George is interesting: the winning of The Ashes

Part 2

England Past

Chapter 2

John Wesley & the 18th Century

'John Wesley was one of the architects of modern England.
He created a new Church and helped to build a new nation.'
Roy Hattersley

JOHN WESLEY AND THE 18TH CENTURY

Morality and religion have collapsed to a degree that has never been known in any Christian country. Our prospect is very terrible and the symptoms grow worse from day to day. The accumulating torrent of evil threatens a general inundation and destruction of these realms.

You could have been forgiven for thinking that this was a leader from a recent Daily Telegraph, but it was in fact written by Bishop Berkeley in his *Discourse to Magistrates and Men in Authority* in 1738. England in the 18th century witnessed a great exodus from the country to the towns and cities, resulting in cramped, squalid urban conditions. The rumblings of the Industrial Revolution could already be heard and the moral state of the nation was in disarray. In continental Europe, the seeds of revolution could be discerned, as the common people became more disenchanted with ruling elites. It has often been said that it was the influence of John Wesley which averted revolution in our own country.

Wesley, born in 1703, was a Church of England minister who, to his dying day, never wanted schism with the established Church. However, he has long been seen as the father of Methodism and thus began a tradition of non-conformist denominations which includes Baptists, Presbyterians, Congregationalists, Evangelical Free, Apostolics and Pentecostals. These denominations are far stronger than their counterparts on mainland Europe and are a major factor in the comparative strength of the English Church. There is something in the English character which warms to non-conformity, and Wesley, Whitefield and the other leaders of the Evangelical awakening in the late 18th century made dissent respectable.

The Christian foundations of the nation were strengthened through the ministry of the Wesleys, at a time when its moral health was at a very low point. In contrast with the England of today, the subject of personal faith was freely discussed in public, a shared Christian consensus underpinning everyday life. True, there were many who disliked Evangelicals like Wesley and Whitefield, preferring a quieter, more private creed and this high church Anglican tradition is still alive and well.

John Wesley preached in the open air, because many chapels and churches would not yield their pulpits to him. The spiritual airwaves were open and explaining the gospel of salvation to grimy miners in the market place was perfectly acceptable: permission did not have to be sought from the local council. Although Wesley was vitally concerned with appalling living conditions, alcoholism and poverty, he realised that to change behaviour you had to change men's hearts; unlike Mary Whitehouse centuries later, whose tinkering with the symptoms of malaise was like swatting flies rather than getting rid of the carcass.

The genius of Methodism was that it tapped in to an aspect of the national character - a penchant for organisation. The English like nothing better than to organise, or to be organised; we crave structure. Wesley developed Methodist societies, preaching circuits, printing presses, the latter funding much of his church activities. The first Methodist Conference took place in 1744 and by this time much of the structures of current Methodism were in place.

Welfare Pioneer

Although most remembered for his 250,000 miles on horseback preaching in the open air, Wesley was also one of the founding fathers of the social care which eventually became the Welfare State of post-war Britain. He sets out the principles of his philanthropy in his sermon on *The Use of Money*, where he urges his hearers to be entrepreneurial... *'gain all you can, save all you can, and give all you can'*. He preached this sermon twenty three times and it is not fanciful to suggest that the roots of the great philanthropic movements of Victorian times can be traced back to Wesley and others. There is a great charitable tradition in this country - more of this in the chapter on Philanthropy - and Wesley's methodical, organised approach to giving was a major contributor.

Wesley was also a passionate believer in the importance of education for all, regardless of wealth, social standing or age. He founded many schools and the various bands, classes and societies of Methodism became important educational channels as well as developing spirituality. He was a prolific author who believed passionately in the educational value of the printed word. He spent a great deal of time visiting the sick and developed an interest in medicine. With the assistance of a qualified surgeon and pharmacist, Wesley began offering medical treatment to the poor, solemnly resolving that he would not go beyond his own knowledge.

A zealous preacher, teacher, social reformer and theologian, Wesley's influence is still powerful today in helping shape many of the institutions of today. I will let Roy Hattersley have the last word: *'Had Wesley done no more than found the Methodist Church, he would have deserved a place in the pantheon of great Englishmen. He was one of the architects of modern England. John Wesley's Second Reformation created a new Church and helped to build a new nation.'*

William Wilberforce & The Clapham Sect

In 1785 Wilberforce underwent a conversion experience and became an evangelical Christian, resulting in major changes to his lifestyle and a lifelong concern for reform. He describes his life's work thus: *'God Almighty has set before me two great objects, the suppression of the slave trade and the reformation of manners (morality).'* He supported campaigns such as the Society for Suppression of Vice, British missionary work in India, the creation of a free colony in Sierra Leone, the foundation of the Church Mission Society and the Society for the Prevention of Cruelty to Animals.

Wilberforce and his friends were part of the upper class, aristocrats who were not interested in changing the structure of society per se. If some 'Christian' biographers are to be believed, the members of the Clapham Sect were almost divine and Clifford Hill, in particular, is guilty of a lack of objectivity. For example, Wilberforce's innate conservatism led him to support politically and socially repressive legislation, and resulted in criticism that he was ignoring injustices at home while campaigning for the enslaved abroad. He did not support trades unions, nor did he support women's rights.

Wilberforce was a man of great personal charm. Privately, in his diary, he agonised about his backsliding, his time-wasting or his failure to pray, but with his friends he was always gregarious, a wonderful conversationalist, the life and soul of the party. William Hague tells endearing stories about Wilberforce's chaotic lack of organisation, his mountains of unanswered correspondence, the sacks full of letters which he would drag around with him to answer. His house was filled with guests all day long, and people queued to see him in the street.

In later years, Wilberforce supported the campaign for the complete abolition of slavery, and continued his involvement after 1826, when he resigned from Parliament because of his failing health. That campaign led to the Slavery Abolition Act 1833, which abolished slavery in most of the British Empire; Wilberforce died just three days after hearing that the passage of the Act through Parliament was assured. He was buried in Westminster Abbey, close to his friend William Pitt.

Wilberforce was generous with his time and money, believing that those with wealth had a duty to give a significant portion of their income to the needy. Yearly, he gave away thousands of pounds, much of it to clergymen to distribute in their parishes. He paid off the debts of others, supported education and missions, and in a year of food shortages gave to charity more than his own yearly income. He was exceptionally hospitable, and could not bear to dismiss any of his servants: as a result, his home was full of old and incompetent servants!

Chapter 3

The Victorians

'The Missionaries must be men of great piety, prudence, courage, and forbearance.'

William Carey

THE VICTORIANS

William Carey: Father of Missions

Generally acknowledged as the father of the modern missionary movement, Carey was by trade a shoemaker, largely self-taught and with exceptional linguistic gifts; he devoted himself to the study of Sanskrit, Bengali, Hindustani, and other native tongues. His excellence made it possible for him to become Professor of Sanskrit and Bengali in Fort William College, Calcutta, at a salary of 500 rupees a month. It is evidence of his selflessness that he devoted his entire salary to the work of spreading the gospel, keeping only a small portion for necessary expenses.

For forty-one years Carey was the recognised leader of the growing Indian Mission, a man of great versatility, pioneering in agriculture, horticulture, and in the promotion of vernacular education. He was the moving spirit of the Serampore Trio who set up and operated the first steam engine in India, introduced the large scale manufacture of paper, established the great Mission Press, and built a college which still stands to train Christian leaders. He was interested in social reform as an expression of the Christian spirit and used his influence against suttee (widow burning) and the practice of casting babies into the Ganges as a sacrifice to the gods. It was Carey who founded the Christian Church in India, and, with the help of associates, translated and printed the Bible into 34 different tongues.

Carey, in the first and still greatest missionary treatise in the English language, horribly titled *An Enquiry into the Obligations of Christians to use Means for the Conversion of the Heathens*, sets out qualifications for missionaries:

The Missionaries must be men of great piety, prudence, courage, and forbearance; of undoubted orthodoxy in their sentiments, and must enter with all their hearts into the spirit of their mission; they must be willing to leave all the comforts of life behind them, and to encounter all the hardships of a torrid or a frigid climate, an uncomfortable manner of living, and every other inconvenience that can attend this undertaking. They must ....gain some acquaintance with the language of the natives (for which purpose two would be better than one), and by all lawful means to endeavour to cultivate a friendship with them, and as soon as possible let them know the errand for which they were sent. They must endeavour to convince them that it was their good alone which induced them to forsake their friends, and all the comforts of their native country.

It might likewise be of importance, if God should bless their labours, for them to encourage any appearances of gifts amongst the people of their charge; if such should be raised up many advantages would be derived from their knowledge of the language and customs of their countrymen; and their change of conduct would give great weight to their ministrations.

Unity

The Serampore Trio of Carey, Marshman and Ward were unique: not only did they conform to these qualifications for missionaries, there existed between them an extraordinary unity which sustained them through many difficult years. Their hearts beat as one, their vision identical and this was the secret of their achievements in opening up the subcontinent for the Gospel. They did much to shape the English character in making the service of others a key constituent. They went to India to serve the Indian people as equals, not as with the East India Company to extract resources and wealth from the people. The Serampore Trio changed history.

George Müller

The work of Müller and his wife with orphans began in 1836 with the preparation of their own home at 6 Wilson Street, Bristol for the accommodation of thirty girls. In 1845, as growth continued, Müller decided that a separate building designed to house 300 children was necessary, and in 1849, at Ashley Down, Bristol, that home opened. By 1870, more than 2,000 children were being accommodated in five homes.

Through all this, Müller never made requests for financial support, nor did he go into debt, even though the five homes cost over £100,000 to build. He often received unsolicited food donations only hours before they were needed to feed the children, further strengthening his faith. The children were educated and well-dressed and Müller even employed a school inspector to maintain high standards. In 1871 an article in The Times stated that since 1836, 23,000 children had been educated in the schools and very many thousands had been educated in other schools, but funded by the orphanage. The article also states that since its founding, 64,000 Bibles, 85,000 Testaments and 29,000,000 religious books had been issued and distributed.

In 1875, at the age of seventy, Müller began a seventeen year period of missionary travel. In that time, he preached in the United States, India, Australia, Japan, China, and nearly forty other countries. He travelled over 200,000 miles, and his language abilities allowed him to preach in English, French, and German. His sermons were translated into over a dozen other languages and in 1892 he returned to England, where he died on March 10, 1898.

Lord Shaftesbury - 'Righteousness Exalteth a Nation'

The seventh Earl of Shaftesbury, Lord Ashley, had a profound effect on the social and religious life of the nation during Victorian times. His influence gave rise to dozens of voluntary organisations still operating today which made England a kinder and more caring society. A dour introvert, Shaftesbury was not the life and soul of the party. His acute sense of his shortcomings drove him to work unstintingly on behalf of the oppressed and marginalised; his faith and politics were inseparable and he often took on powerful vested interests. He was not popular with the rich and privileged, but thousands of ordinary folk turned out for his funeral.

He was operating within a broadly shared Christian consensus: 49 per cent of English people could be found in church on a Sunday morning in the mid 19th century. This key factor was influential in enabling him to get so many new laws onto the statute book. One hundred and fifty years later, this consensus has collapsed, although some of Shaftesbury's values live on: the Shaftesbury Society, which he founded in 1844, still to this day helps the poor, disabled and marginalised.

Christianity was a major opponent of the march of capitalism in the 1840s & 1850s: Jesus taught that you cannot serve God and Mammon. A nation that had modelled itself on the socio-economic ideas of Bentham and Malthus had enthroned Money and it was not surprising that it should lose its sense of God. In an era known for double standards - amongst Christians, as much as anyone

- this opposition to rampant capitalist excess often took the form of charity. Some capitalists were candid enough to recognise that the greedy logic of their belief in laissez-faire economics was incompatible with a Christian witness. Others, perhaps the majority, lived with this contradiction, being quite happy to state that they believed the working class were made in God's image, while treating them as severely as slaves on Caribbean sugar plantations.

It is interesting to note that many of the societies and institutions founded in the Victorian era live on today, but many have come adrift from their spiritual moorings. This may or may not be a good thing, depending on your point of view. Football clubs like Southampton and Celtic started life as Church football teams; the Young Men's Christian Association (YMCA) has re-invented itself as a primarily 'secular' institution with faith no longer a major factor. The Shaftesbury Society itself, although acknowledging its roots, operates as a mainstream charity where personal faith is not a requirement for employees.

Gladstone

William Gladstone, in his early years, was of the Evangelical persuasion, which has never sat easily with the English character. Peter Ackroyd makes the point that understatement is a central feature of the English character and it is no surprise, therefore, that the emphasis on a personal faith and religious experience central to evangelicalism should not find fertile soil in England. Gladstone himself gradually moved away from the evangelical fervour of his youth toward the high churchmanship which he espoused in later life and which informed much of his political thought. He was famously at odds with Queen Victoria for much of his career and she once complained, '*He always addresses me as if I were a public meeting.*'

Gladstone published his first book, *The State in its Relations with the Church*, in 1838, in which he argued that the goal of the state should be to promote and defend the interests of the Church of England. He was a man who continually struggled to reconcile his faith to his actions, and through his meticulous diary keeping we are allowed to peer through a large window into his soul. A statesman of great energy and forcefulness of character, he strove to realise God's purposes, as he saw them, in the twisting and slippery paths of public service.

There are many biographies of the statesman. Roy Jenkins, in an otherwise superb study of the great man, seems to categorise Gladstone's struggles with personal sin as flights of eccentricity and delusion rather than a common feature of Christian life through the ages. He regarded his subject as 'priggish' in his attitude to the ways of the world but Jenkins, not sharing his subject's personal faith, simply doesn't attempt to understand it.

Gladstone founded the deliciously titled Church Penitentiary Association for the Reclamation of Fallen Women. In May 1849 he began his most active 'rescue work' with 'fallen women' and met prostitutes late at night on the street, in his house or in their houses, helpfully writing their names in a private notebook. He aided the House of Mercy near Windsor and spent much time arranging employment for ex-prostitutes. In 1927, during a court case over published claims that he had had improper relationships with some of these women, the jury unanimously found that the evidence '*completely vindicated the high moral character of the late*

Mr. W. E. Gladstone'. Much to the criticism of his peers, he continued this practice even after he was elected Prime Minister.

However, Gladstone's impact on the nation was not primarily in the field of social work: he left a lasting legacy on the politics, finance and institutions of England, especially in the role of Chancellor. Liberal Prime Minister four times, more than anyone else, he was 84 years old when he resigned for the last time, making him Britain's oldest Prime Minister. He also served as Chancellor of the Exchequer four times. The Austrian economist, Joseph Schumpeter, described Gladstone's approach to finance in his *History of Economic Analysis:*

> *In 1848... there was one man who knew how to turn budgets into political triumphs and who stands in history as the greatest English financier of economic liberalism, Gladstone... The greatest feature of Gladstonian finance... was that it translated a social, political, and economic vision into the clauses of a set of co-ordinated fiscal measures... Gladstonian finance was the finance of the system of 'natural liberty', laissez-faire, and free trade... the most important thing was to remove fiscal obstructions to private activity. And since the profit motive and the propensity to save were considered of paramount importance for the economic progress of all classes, this meant in particular that taxation should as little as possible interfere with the net earnings of business... As regards indirect taxes, the principle of least interference was interpreted by Gladstone to mean that taxation should be concentrated on a few important articles, leaving the rest free... Last, but not least, we have the principle of the balanced budget.*

Redistribution of Wealth

During his terms of office as Chancellor, Gladstone earned the reputation as the liberator of British trade and the working man's breakfast table, the man responsible for the emancipation of the popular press from *'taxes upon knowledge'* and for introducing a tax on the succession of the estates of the rich. This latter measure has been responsible over many years for redistributing the fruits of the capitalist system more equitably. Gladstone's popularity rested on his taxation policies which meant to his supporters balance, social equity and political justice. Nigel Lawson, one of Margaret Thatcher's Chancellors, believed Gladstone to be the *'greatest Chancellor of all time'*.

Lloyd George said of Gladstone in 1915:

> *What a man he was! Head and shoulders above anyone else I have ever seen in the House of Commons. I did not like him much. He hated Nonconformists and Welsh Nonconformists in particular, and he had no real sympathy with the working-classes. But he was far and away the best Parliamentary speaker I have ever heard.*

And Asquith in 1922:

> *Gladstone was the most faithful and enlightened steward there has ever been of our national finance. He abhorred waste. He preferred the remission of burdensome taxation even to the diminution of the public debt. He never faltered in his allegiance to the cause of setting free the smaller nationalities, crushed between the upper and the nether millstone of arrogant and militant autocracies. He was the pioneer in the long, arduous, still uncompleted struggle, in the international sphere, of right against might, of freedom against force.*

A few days after he relinquished the premiership, Gladstone wrote to George William Erskine Russell on 6 March 1894:

Of one thing I am, and always have been, convinced - it is not by the State that man can be regenerated, and the terrible woes of this darkened world effectually dealt with. I am not so much afraid of Democracy or of Science as of the love of money. This seems to me to be a growing evil. Also, there is a danger from the growth of that dreadful military spirit.

Prophetic words indeed.

Chapter 4

Philanthropy

'If ever there came among men what they call the Christianity of Christ, it was in the message of Dickens.'

G. K. Chesterton

Philanthropy can be defined as the provision of financial, material, and ideal resources for cultural, social, and educational institutions. Charity organization movements were one of the key characteristics of Victorian era philanthropists. With the emergence of nation states prior to and during this period, poverty and social welfare gradually became embodied in law, although State reform was often highly bureaucratic and humiliating to the poor who received aid. Civil and religious structures for taking care of the poor began to mix, resulting in a more bureaucratic and regimented approach to philanthropy.

> *There is a time when a Christian must sell all and give to the poor, as they did in the Apostles times. There is a time allsoe when Christians (though they give not all yet) must give beyond their abillity, as they of Macedonia, Cor. 2, 6. Likewise community of perills calls for extraordinary liberality, and soe doth community in some speciall service for the Churche. Lastly, when there is no other means whereby our Christian brother may be relieved in his distress, we must help him beyond our abillity rather than tempt God in putting him upon help by miraculous or extraordinary meanes.*

John Winthrop
A Modell of Christian Charity (1630)

The 19th century is often described as the golden age of philanthropy and was often, but not exclusively, based on religious tradition that was centuries in the making. The church increasingly became the vehicle of private and public social work and although philanthropy was rooted in religious and church tradition, it also spread outside the church. Much that is good about England today is a direct result of the foundations put in place during Victorian times. Charity and welfare are part of the English DNA and our generosity and championing of the underdog have been centuries in the making.

Self Help

The moralising concept of self-help seemed to be a value prized by the mid-Victorian middle class: whereas 'self-help' strengthened the individual, charity enfeebled him or her. Extending the notion of self-help to the working class lifted a load from the shoulders of the middle class, letting them rest easy with the fruits of their own achievements. It was thus up to the working class to make provision for their own welfare.

The Co-operative Movement began in Rochdale in 1844 and was initially a trading association which provided goods (and later services) at a reasonable price, with a dividend paid to the members of the 'co-operative'. Friendly Societies were also attempts at creating groups of like-minded friends, neighbours or work-mates who would pool a certain amount of money, on a weekly basis, and thus have a reserve fund in case of unforeseen disaster. Membership reached 925,000 in 1815. The Manchester Unity of Oddfellows was the largest Friendly Society.

During the first half of the 19th century, it was often claimed that poverty was the result of an individual's inability to cope with life, linked to some defect, like laziness or alcohol dependency. It was felt that the deserving poor should be encouraged to help themselves out of their predicament through hard work, abstemious behaviour, thrift and godliness. The role of Government was limited: doling out large sums of relief to the poor would only have the perverse effect of encouraging poverty, especially among the undeserving.

Poverty

Henry Mayhew (*London Labour and the London Poor*, 1851) wrote newspaper articles describing the abject living conditions of some of the more colourful characters among the London poor. It appeared to him that those living on or below the breadline were not all guilty of some moral defect. Many were simply unable to find sufficiently well-paid employment and his work influenced writers such as Dickens. Progress towards the idea of 'human rights' and the role of the state in the well-being of the individual was slow. The familiar question was how to balance the uplifting of the poor with the distribution of material relief, which might be seen to reward those unwilling to make efforts themselves. And within the working class itself, even if the moral dimension was often absent, there was still a feeling on occasions that industrious workers should not have to subsidise lazy, marginal characters.

Awareness about poverty in late Victorian Britain was helped by Seebohm Rowntree's study of poverty in York in 1899 (*Poverty : A Study of Town Life*, 1901) : he pointed out that the majority of the working class could expect to experience poverty a number of times in their lives, when young, when having children and when old. Drink and gambling were seen to exacerbate the problems and survival was conditional on workers avoiding these traps. Rowntree defined the poverty line as *'a standard of bare subsistence rather than living'*. According to him, 10 per cent of the population lived in *'primary poverty'* and another 18 per cent earned more, but wasted their extra money on wasteful vices. A major problem concerned large families who had only a relatively low income. The more children they had, the more they were penalised.

Josephine Butler campaigned on behalf of the hundreds of destitute and poverty stricken women she had met who had turned to prostitution as the only way out of desperate poverty. From 1869 until 1883 Butler dedicated herself to this work, campaigning for the repeal of the Contagious Diseases Act which criminalised prostitutes rather than those who paid them. Almost half a century before Butler was born, another Christian woman was starting a lifetime of service to the imprisoned and the homeless. Elizabeth Fry was a Quaker and an evangelistic preacher of great repute. The appalling state of prisons and the particular ill treatment of women prisoners led Fry to devote much of her time to the welfare and well being of prisoners as well as setting up one of London's first night shelters for the homeless in 1820.

The Chocolate Trinity

There were a group of Quaker industrialists who are often called The Chocolate Trinity: George Cadbury, Joseph Rowntree and Joseph Storrs Fry. Cadbury's faith was his primary motivation, and the fulfilment of its commandments, his over-riding objective. He improved the living conditions of thousands, influenced legislation, created models for future industry and became a catalyst for social change. His efforts also saw many come to faith, perhaps his most valuable legacy. His biographer notes that: *'He had only one passion - to leave the world a better place than he found it - and he spent his whole life in its pursuit.'*

Joseph Rowntree (1836-1925) was both an active Quaker and also a hugely successful businessman. As a young man he took over his father's grocery shop in York but it was in the confectionery industry that Rowntree was to become a household name. Rowntree's legacy, however, spreads far beyond the popularity today of fruit pastilles and fruit gums. Indeed, Rowntree's most important influence is that of a faith-inspired entrepreneur, a progressive industrial patriarch with a deep social conscience, who had a far reaching, positive influence upon Victorian England. Today, the values and motivations of Rowntree live on, embodied in the Trusts he established, influencing the world beyond the limits of his lifetime. His biographer described him as *'an adventurer to the end of life, forever peering forward, never content with what had been achieved…. He heard the echoes from the past, and with them he challenged the future.'*

The third of the Chocolate Trinity was Joseph Storrs Fry II. Born into a Quaker household, Fry became a third generation confectioner, inheriting the chairmanship of J S Fry and Son, Britain's largest chocolate and cocoa manufacturer. Fry's accounted for a quarter of the chocolate sold in Britain. The family concern had developed a reputation for innovation, quality and honesty, all hallmarks of Quaker industrial practice which was distinctive during this era. Each of them sought to enable those who worked for them by giving them dignity and meaning to their work and life and leisure. Their desire to serve God as their motivation was unapologetic and unashamed; great lives lived in the service of others, examples of men and women who have taken seriously Christ's urging and have through their work reflected God's purposes.

Dame Cecily Saunders founded the Hospice movement, who declared that without the inspiration of Jesus' teaching and the strength given her by His Spirit, the problems she faced would have overwhelmed her. Her work has spread worldwide, whilst in Oxford in 1892 the first British hospice for children was founded in Oxford by dedicated Anglican nuns.

Andrew Carnegie was a self-made man, extremely rich by the age of 40. He set his own philanthropic agenda, notably his libraries programme which was his original solution to the lack of educational opportunities in the late 1800s and which by-passed the existing charitable sector of his day. By the nineteen twenties he had also become a major supporter of adult education. Lord Beaverbrook, a Scottish Canadian, gave the bulk of his huge fortune for the establishment of scholarships at the university of his native New Brunswick, and to the establishment of the Beaverbrook Art Gallery.

No doubt, at the heart of these stories of Scottish philanthropists there lurks some essentially religious idea of life. Certainly, Carnegie and Beaverbrook believed they owed their success not only to their own prodigious energy but to Providence; and that, having obeyed the divine ordinance to work while there was yet day, they also must obey the injunction never to forget the poor man at the gate.

The Church - Agent of Social Care

Philanthropically-funded hygiene efforts, such as campaigning for clean air and building public bath-houses were logical responses to urgent needs of the day, given the dirt and squalor in which much of the population lived, not to mention frequent epidemics of infectious disease. Prevalent in the Victorian period was the distinction between the deserving and non-deserving poor, and the official approach to providing poor relief had been designed to force that distinction. There was strong support in the belief that providing too much relief, or making it too easy to obtain, would encourage many of the working classes to choose to become dependent upon it. Hence, in part the gaunt and severely regimental management of the workhouses.

Bleak House

Although famous as a great novelist, Charles Dickens campaigned tirelessly against poverty throughout most of the first half of the 19th century. As he grew older, his work demonstrated a growing pessimism, and dealt with the larger, more insoluble issues than the specific social ills of his previous novels. He used satire to expose the hypocrisy of Victorian institutions, as well as the 'do-gooders' who were so bound up in their self-righteous charitable acts that they failed to see the poverty and suffering immediately before them. He gave as much to individuals whose destitution moved him as he did to organizations and committees that assisted the poor and belonged to and advised many of these same committees and organizations. Dickens spoke in support of the community hospitals which had been established to give assistance to those who could not afford medical attention; he financially assisted and provided instruction for the newly established Ragged schools, which were public institutions erected for the improvement of impoverished children.

He is steeped, as many Victorian writers were, in the knowledge, the words, the stories, the rhetoric, the practices of the national Church, although he had an intense distaste of the hierarchical and authoritarian tendencies of much of organised religion, with a special dislike of Rome. The hectoring, moralising tone of a certain strand of muscular Evangelicalism was distasteful to him and he was firmly on the side of the poor. Wherever he was, in London, in Europe, in America, he was drawn to Christian assemblies; sermon-tasting was what he did a lot of on Sundays. He was baptized conventionally into the Church of England, and, like his beloved sister Fanny, was sent regularly to church. Church of England on Sunday morning, chapel on Sunday evening.

The representation of Christianity in Charles Dickens' works was largely overlooked by his contemporaries, because he did not espouse the views of the Established Church; indeed, he often portrayed Church officials in a negative light in order to highlight the hypocrisies he saw in the established Church. He wanted to remove religion from the high Church and place it back into the lives of the common people. Dickens believed that it was his responsibility as a writer to illustrate the failings of society as an *'absence'* from the teachings of Christ. He intensely disliked the Victorian tendency to moralise and often used allegory to make his points.

G. K. Chesterton, who famously said *'if there was no God, there would be no atheists'*, said of Dickens:

> *If ever there was a message full of what modern people call true Christianity, the direct appeal to the common heart, a faith that was simple, a hope that was infinite, and a charity that was omnivorous, if ever there came among men what they call the Christianity of Christ, it was in the message of Dickens*

The Lady with the Lamp

> *God called me in morning and asked me would I do good for him alone without reputation*

Inspired by what she took as a divine calling, Florence Nightingale announced her decision to enter nursing in 1845, despite the intense anger and distress of her family, particularly her mother. In this, she rebelled against the expected role for a woman of her status, which was to become a wife and mother. Nightingale worked hard to educate herself in the art and science of nursing, in spite of opposition from her family and the restrictive social code for affluent young English women. She became the leading advocate for improved medical care in the infirmaries and immediately engaged the support of Charles Villiers, then president of the Poor Law Board. This led to her active role in the reform of the Poor Laws, extending far beyond the provision of medical care.

As the Lady with the Lamp, ministering to the wounded and dying of the Crimean War, she offers an enduring image of sentimental appeal and one that is permanently lodged in our national consciousness. But the awesome scale of her achievements over the course of her ninety years is infinitely more inspiring than this mythical simplification. The sentimental legend has it that she was a ministering angel and a nurse, but she was never a nurse, except in a very limited sense: she was a great nursing theoretician. She was one of the most important statistical pioneers of the 19th century, and one of the greatest gifts she had was to imagine herself in situations, and with a certain amount of statistical material, work out solutions. The range of young Florence's intellectual pursuits is awe-inspiring. A classicist and linguist, she was also keenly interested in theology and a gifted mathematician.

Her most famous contribution was during the Crimean War, which became her central focus when reports began to filter back to Britain about the horrific conditions for the wounded. On October 21, 1854 Nightingale and a staff of thirty eight women volunteer nurses, trained by Nightingale and including her aunt Mai Smith, were sent to the Crimea, with the authorisation of Sidney Herbert. At Scutari Nightingale and her nurses found wounded soldiers being badly cared for by overworked medical staff in the face of official indifference. Medicines were in short supply, hygiene was being neglected, and mass infections were common, many of them fatal. There was no equipment to process food for the patients.

Nightingale and her compatriots began by thoroughly cleaning the hospital and equipment, and reorganising patient care. Although she met resistance from the doctors and officers, her changes vastly improved conditions for the wounded and by April mortality rates had dropped by 40 per cent to just 2 per cent.

Nightingale's work inspired massive public support throughout England, where she was celebrated and admired as 'The Lady of The Lamp' after the Grecian lamp she always carried in her tireless evening and night-time visits to injured soldiers. Nightingale's lamp also allowed her to work late every night, maintaining meticulous medical records for the hospital, and writing personal letters to the family of every soldier who died in the hospital. She is remembered today because of the compassion, care and administrative skills that she introduced to the profession of nursing, to patient care and to the maintenance of medical records. The depth of her commitment to the care of her patients in Crimea earned her the everlasting respect and affection of the common soldier.

The Salvation Army

In 1865 William and Catherine Booth founded the Whitechapel Christian Mission in London's East End to help feed and house the poor. The mission was reorganised in 1878 along military lines, with the preachers known as officers and Booth as the General. After this the group became known as the Salvation Army and William Booth sought to bring into his worship services an informal atmosphere that would encourage new converts. Joyous singing, instrumental music, clapping of hands and an invitation to repent characterised Salvation Army meetings.

Early in his career, the tall, gaunt Evangelist halted outside The Blind Beggar Tavern up the Mile End Road, East London. *'There is a heaven in East London for everyone,'* he cried, *'for everyone who will stop and think and look to Christ as a personal saviour.'* From the pub came a volley of jeers and oaths, followed by a rotten egg. The preacher made his way through savage fighting men, ragged match-sellers, orange-women, and Irish flower girls clad only in soiled petticoats with their bare feet covered in dirt; he strode past crowded tenements and stinking alleys where the sick and dying lay side by side.

William Booth was deeply influenced by his wife, who believed that women were equal to men and it was only inadequate education and social custom that made them men's intellectual inferiors. She was an inspiring speaker and helped to promote the idea of women preachers. The Salvation Army gave women equal responsibility with men for preaching and welfare work and on one occasion William Booth remarked that: *'My best men are women!'*

It was not until 1878 when The Christian Mission changed its name to The Salvation Army that things began to happen.

The impetus changed and the Army began to grow; Booth's fiery sermons and sharp imagery motivated many to leave their past behind and start a new life as a soldier in The Salvation Army. The Booths helped prepare England for the Welfare State, although they met with tremendous opposition. They are part of that great heritage of kind-heartedness and tolerance for which the English are renowned and, although to 21st century eyes they seem highly authoritarian, perhaps their methods are preferable to the bureaucratic nightmare currently encountered by those seeking benefits.

Charles Booth (no relation to William) wrote *The Life and Labour of the People in London*, 1902: he noticed an *'arithmetic of woe'*, with over 30 per cent of the population of London living in poverty. He did not agree with the idea that the poor were totally responsible for their predicament. He carried out a careful classification of the population and his findings showed that problems linked to employment were at the heart of poverty - rather than any innate immorality. At the end of the 19th century it was clear that although it would be wrong to claim that the majority of the population lived in absolute poverty, the majority of the population lived in the shadow of poverty. They had little in the way of savings or insurance to protect themselves from any sudden disaster - illness, death, or loss of employment.

A young medical student, Thomas Barnardo, who helped Booth at indoor meetings, departed to devote his life to the rescue of homeless children. *'You look after the children and I'll look after the adults,'* were Booth's final words.

Doctor Barnardo

Doctor Thomas John Barnardo (1845-1905) is a classically Victorian figure - evangelical, entrepreneurial and philanthropic. His crusade to *'rescue children from the streets'* was one the best known social interventions in the last half of the 19th century and he became a strongly evangelical Christian *'impatient to convert others, urgent for action'*. In the short space of forty years, starting without patronage or influence of any kind, he raised the sum of three and a quarter million pounds, established a network of Homes for the reception, care and training of homeless, needy and afflicted children.

He shared a number of qualities with other charismatic founders of philanthropic organizations - a belief in the rightness of his actions and his analysis; the ability to network and to present his work in ways that opened purse strings. The entrepreneurialism of Dr Barnardo finds an echo in many youth, community and voluntary organisations in which informal educators function.

Chapter 5

God's Funeral

'Perhaps only those who have known the peace of God which passes all understanding can have any conception of what was lost when Western Europe began to discard Christianity.'

A. N. Wilson

GOD'S FUNERAL

I

I saw a slowly-stepping train --
Lined on the brows, scoop-eyed and bent and hoar --
Following in files across a twilit plain
A strange and mystic form the foremost bore.

II

And by contagious throbs of thought
Or latent knowledge that within me lay
And had already stirred me, I was wrought
To consciousness of sorrow even as they.

III

The fore-borne shape, to my blurred eyes,
At first seemed man-like, and anon to change
To an amorphous cloud of marvellous size,
At times endowed with wings of glorious range.

IV

And this phantasmal variousness
Ever possessed it as they drew along:
Yet throughout all it symboled none the less
Potency vast and loving-kindness strong.

V

Almost before I knew I bent
Towards the moving columns without a word;
They, growing in bulk and numbers as they went,
Struck out sick thoughts that could be overheard: --

VI

'O man-projected Figure, of late
Imaged as we, thy knell who shall survive?
Whence came it we were tempted to create
One whom we can no longer keep alive?

VII

'Framing him jealous, fierce, at first,
We gave him justice as the ages rolled,
Will to bless those by circumstance accurst,
And longsuffering, and mercies manifold.

VIII

'And, tricked by our own early dream
And need of solace, we grew self-deceived,
Our making soon our maker did we deem,
And what we had imagined we believed,

IX

'Till, in Time's stayless stealthy swing,
Uncompromising rude reality
Mangled the Monarch of our fashioning,
Who quavered, sank; and now has ceased to be.

X

'So, toward our myth's oblivion,
Darkling, and languid-lipped, we creep and grope
Sadlier than those who wept in Babylon,
Whose Zion was a still abiding hope.

XI

'How sweet it was in years far hied
To start the wheels of day with trustful prayer,
To lie down liegely at the eventide
And feel a blest assurance he was there!

XII

'And who or what shall fill his place?
Whither will wanderers turn distracted eyes
For some fixed star to stimulate their pace
Towards the goal of their enterprise?'...

XIII

Some in the background then I saw,
Sweet women, youths, men, all incredulous,
Who chimed as one: 'This figure is of straw,
This requiem mockery! Still he lives to us!'

XIV

I could not prop their faith: and yet
Many I had known: with all I sympathized;
And though struck speechless, I did not forget
That what was mourned for, I, too, once had prized.

XV

Still, how to bear such loss I deemed
The insistent question for each animate mind,
And gazing, to my growing sight there seemed
A pale yet positive gleam low down behind,

XVI

Whereof, to lift the general night,
A certain few who stood aloof had said,
'See you upon the horizon that small light --
Swelling somewhat?' Each mourner shook his head.

XVII

And they composed a crowd of whom
Some were right good, and many nigh the best....
Thus dazed and puzzled 'twixt the gleam and gloom
Mechanically I followed with the rest.

Thomas Hardy
God's Funeral

It seems odd to be talking about 'God's funeral' hard on the
heels of so much vigorous Christianity in action during the
mid and late Victorian era. The rose is surely in full bloom,
vigorous and apparently in rude health: below the surface,
however, the roots are under increasing attack. It is in the

realm of ideas that we can detect the changes which, a century later, would lead to the Sixties Revolution and abandonment of the Christian framework and values.

It is extraordinary that the century that witnessed the greatest period of church-building in human history, the mass revivals of the Evangelicals and the Anglo-Catholics and the founding of missionary societies, should also have been the period when atheism went from being an esoteric and secretive persuasion to becoming, as G. K. Chesterton described it, *'the religion of the suburbs'*. By the start of the 20th century the great mass of thinking men and women had started to abandon the religion which, for at least a millennium, had dominated the British Isles.

Philosophers are often anonymous figures, unknown to the vast majority of citizens but whose influence casts a long and powerful shadow. Men and women of ideas were, to borrow a hackneyed modern phrase, starting to think *outside the box*. The 'box' was essentially the Christian consensus, grooved in through centuries of Christian theology, practice, Church history and doxology: great hymns poured from the pens of hymn writers like Isaac Watts and Charles Wesley, reinforcing a shared world-view with memorable tunes and simple, orthodox theology. The man in the street would be hard pressed to name the influential philosophers of the day: Hume, Kant, Carlyle, Hegel, Comte, Mill et al. But it is in the milieu of ideas that revolutionary thoughts were debated and doubts about the existence of the Almighty expressed.

A. N. Wilson puts it thus:

> *Perhaps only those who have known the peace of God which passes all understanding can have any conception of what was lost between one hundred and one hundred and fifty*

*years ago when the human race in Western Europe began
to discard Christianity. The loss was not merely an
intellectual change, the discarding of one proposition in
favour of another. Indeed, though many intellectual
justifications were offered by those who lost faith, the
process would seem to have been, in many cases, just as
emotional as religious conversion; and its roots were often
quite as irrational. In all the inner journeys which ended
with 'God's funeral' for the believer, there was potential for
profound agony. This is the story of bereavement as much
as adventure. This devastating sense of emotional loss
extends to our own times*

As we examine the ideas of some of the thinkers who
challenged Christian orthodoxy, we can see that the
'invisible worm that flies in the night' of Blake's poem is
starting to poison the roots of the rose. Many are not
celebrating upsetting the apple-cart, but rather there is a
sense of reluctance to demolish cherished shibboleths,
coupled with a poignancy and sadness at what is being lost.
Perhaps there is a subconscious awareness of how far-
reaching the effects of discarding Christianity will be. By
the end of the 19th century, almost all the great writers,
artists, and intellectuals had abandoned Christianity, and
many abandoned belief in God altogether. Echoes of the
'Death of God' could be found practically everywhere: in the
revolutionary politics of Garibaldi and Lenin; in the poetry
of Tennyson and the novels of Hardy; in the work of Freud,
connecting this 'death' to our deepest wishes; and in the
decline of hierarchical male authority and the first stirrings
of feminism.

At the end of the 19th century, Christian theologian Ernst
Troeltsch proclaimed that the sun was setting on
Christianity, and poet Matthew Arnold declared that in the
future poetry would replace religion. The 19th century

provided the context not only for theories of God's demise but also for the numerous challenges that political thinkers, scientists and artists posed to Christian belief. Yet, while the battles between faith and doubt were raging, church attendance did not decline but remained constant. Edward Gibbon's *The History of the Decline and Fall of the Roman Empire*, with its contempt of Christianity's 'highest ideals', and David Hume's sceptical *Dialogues Concerning National Religion*, which challenges the very possibility of the existence of the supernatural, provide the groundwork for the demise of belief in the 19th century.

Further nails in the coffin were George Eliot's translations of *Feuerbach's The Essence of Christianity* and David Friedrich Strauss's *The Life of Jesus, Critically Examined*; Darwin's evolutionary formulations calling into question the idea of a special creation; Marx and Engels's charge that bourgeois institutions used religion to enslave people and make them weak; William James's reading of various religious states in *The Varieties of Religious Experience* as psychological states of mind. Eliot's translations alone introduced into England both Strauss's contentions that the life of Jesus was clothed in myth and Feuerbach's claim that God was nothing more than a projection of humanity's wishes.

Sigmund Freud was clearly fascinated by religion, but thought it would fade into obsolescence as civilization marched forward. The Church of England in particular was devastated by the challenge from its intellectuals and its own wealth and power; by 1900, it was vastly rich, politically and socially powerful, but spiritually empty, however full its pews might have been on a Sunday. God (or man's faith in him) died, but the need to worship remained as a torment to those who thought they had buried Him.

John Stuart Mill

Mill was a strong believer in freedom, especially of speech and of thought. He defended freedom on two grounds. First, he argued, society's utility would be maximized if each person was free to make his or her own choices. Mill believed that freedom was required for each person's development as a whole person. In his famous essay *On Liberty,* Mill enunciated the principle that *'the sole end for which mankind are warranted, individually or collectively, in interfering with the liberty of action of any of their number, is self-protection.'*

David Hume

Hume's *Natural History of Religion* cemented his reputation as a religious sceptic and an atheist, even before its publication. It is an account of the origins and development of religious beliefs, with the thinly disguised agenda of making clear the non-rational origins of religion; primitive peoples devised religion to account for frightening, uncontrollable natural phenomena, such as disease and earthquakes. For Hume, religion is dogmatic and intolerant; worse, it gives rise to theological systems which spread absurdity and intolerance.

Georg Wilhelm Hegel

Arguably the most influential and exciting 19th century philosopher, Hegel doubted the historical accuracy of the gospels and asserted that the Christian religion - and Christ himself - were the products of the communities of faith which produced the Gospels. From this idea of Hegel's and his belief that religion manifests itself in myth, sprang the modern Germanic school of biblical criticism: this critical approach to the scriptures was a major factor in the destruction of ordinary Christian faith in the 19th century.

Charles Darwin

The Origin of Species had been published in 1859 and was to have a profound influence on Western thought. Darwin, a quiet, methodical, homely man, was reluctant to publish his work, sensing that it would pose a major challenge to the notion of God as creator. *'The declining sense of the miraculous'* as Lecky called it in 1863, *'was pushed further into decline by Darwin and the public acceptance of evolution.'* The metaphysical implications of what Darwin painstakingly worked out caused him grief and would undermine traditional theism to the core. Whatever he did or did not do for God, Darwin cut the human race down to size.

Darwin's Theory of Evolution is the widely held notion that all life is related and has descended from a common ancestor: the birds and the bananas, the fishes and the flowers - all related. Darwin's general theory presumes the development of life from non-life and stresses a purely naturalistic (undirected) *'descent with modification'*. That is, complex creatures evolve from more simplistic ancestors naturally over time. In a nutshell, as random genetic mutations occur within an organism's genetic code, the beneficial mutations are preserved because they aid survival - a process known as *'natural selection'*. These beneficial mutations are passed on to the next generation. Over time, beneficial mutations accumulate and the result is an entirely different organism - not just a variation of the original, but an entirely different creature.

The Origin of Species was extremely controversial when published, because the logical extension of Darwin's theory was that homo sapiens was simply another form of animal. It seemed possible that even people might just have evolved - quite possibly from apes - and destroyed the prevailing consensus on how the world was created. Darwin was vehemently attacked, particularly by the Church, but his ideas soon gained currency and have become the new orthodoxy. Those who today hold to the Biblical notion of creation are dismissed as dangerous reactionaries.

Thomas Carlyle

Thomas Carlyle was one of the most influential thinkers of the 19th century. He abandoned orthodox religious belief, and would certainly never pretend to be a Christian, although he went on reading the Bible and concluded that there was something providential in the working of history itself. Carlyle's agonies in print were to become the inner torments, political religious and philosophical, of his generation, which was why he was the greatest of its prophets in the English-speaking world. He mourned his absent Christ and he trembled for a society with no sense of the awesome, no reverence before the great mysteries. Above all, he feared what would happen in a society which plainly could not sustain (morally or politically) a system of oligarchic privilege but which could so easily slither into something worse - anarchy, mayhem, butchery. The notion that the spiritual and political malaise of his times could be solved by parliamentary reforms was ludicrous to him.

John Ruskin, a follower of Carlyle, came to see the 19th century as a nightmare era and the epicentre of the horror was its loss of faith. A stream of books were published which saw religion as a purely human construct and the

Christian religion as an exercise in mythology. Nowadays, such views are commonplace, even amongst the clergy, but in the 19th century they were revolutionary. The idea that Christianity was based on a factual mistake - the mistake of supposing Jesus to be divine - provoked angry reactions from those who believed that Western civilisation was founded on Christ's divinity and the values he gave to the world.

Unbelief

It would be misleading to say that in the 1850s *'atheism was the religion of the suburbs'* as G. K. Chesterton claimed was the case for the next generation. But unbelief was fashionable and widespread. On the surface - at least amongst the middle class - Victorian England still looked like a Christian culture. Churches were still being built and Christian books still published in large numbers. However, beneath the surface deepening cracks were appearing. In academic circles the obsession continued with German philosopher Hegel, described as *'the true philosopher of the modern consciousness'*, with the comment that *'..... the crisis that he was trying to describe was that of a civilisation that has discovered the God upon whom it depended to be also its own creation'*.

Alfred, Lord Tennyson

Poets such as Alfred, Lord Tennyson reflected the immense upheaval taking place in Victorian religious thought, attacking the roots of the sick rose. *'Are God and Nature then at strife?'*, Tennyson asked. This is really the core of 19th century doubt about the Creator: that the God of Scripture and the God discernible from nature violently diverge. The troubled poet saw that the science versus religion debate threatened to remove the religion of the *'inner life'* and wrote *'The churches have killed their Christ.'* Made Poet Laureate by Queen Victoria, he wrote of grief and doubt more than any poet before or since, openly exposing himself to the mood of his age; he absorbed the angst, excitement and triumphs and identified in his poetry with the pre-occupations of the Victorian era.

Reverend H. F. Lyte wrote one of the most haunting lyrics of the 19th century *Abide with Me,* which is still sung at major sporting events in England. Like Tennyson he could have claimed it was the cry of the whole human race. *'I fear no foe with Thee at hand to bless'*… the repeated plea, which has an undoubted pathos, throughout the hymn is that God's Presence will not be removed. This at a time when many, with heavy hearts, were taking leave of God.

Karl Marx

One of Marx's most famous remarks is that *'religion is the opiate of the people'.* He challenged traditional theology and asserted that human beings had created God in their own image; he believed that religion is a response to alienation in material life, and therefore cannot be removed until human material life is emancipated, at which point religion will wither away. Although he was largely ignored by scholars in his own lifetime, his social, economic and political ideas gained rapid acceptance in the socialist movement after his death in 1883. Marx's influence on the history of the 20th century was immense: it is impossible to understand the history of that century without a comprehensive study of Marx's writings; indeed until quite recently almost half the population of the world lived under regimes that claim to be Marxist.

Marx's thought demonstrates strong philosophical influences from Hegel, Jean-Jacques Rousseau and Henri de Saint-Simon; the classical political economy of Adam Smith and David Ricardo; French socialist and sociological thought, in particular Charles Fourier. In 1849 Marx moved to London, where he was to spend the remainder of his life. For a number of years, his family lived in poverty but the wealthier Engels was able to support them to an increasing extent. Gradually, Marx emerged from his political and spiritual isolation and produced his most important body of work, *Das Kapital*. The first volume of this 'Bible of the Working Class' was published in his lifetime, while the remaining volumes were edited by Engels after his friend's death.

Christian Socialism

Charles Kingsley, author of *The Water Babies*, also wrote *Yeast* in 1848, a Christian Socialist novel. In it the young hero has his eyes opened to the plight of the poor and finds himself in London, at St Paul's Cathedral, listening to the choir sing the afternoon service. '*Shall I tell you what they are singing? He hath put down the mighty from their seat, and hath exalted the humble and meek. He hath filled the hungry with good things, and the rich he hath sent empty away.*' These words are delivered to the hero by a mysterious stranger who adds '*No, I dare not despair of you English, as long as I hear your priesthood forced by providence, even in spite of themselves, thus to speak God's words about an age in which the condition of the poor, and the rights and duties of man, are becoming the rallying point for all thought and all organisation.*'

Kingsley espoused the Christian Socialist Movement which was to have a marked effect on the thinking of many English politicians. Roy Hattersley, James Callaghan and Denis Healey are individuals shaped by this way of thinking, albeit in a very English, understated way.

Chapter 6

Sunset of Empire

'Atheism had become the religion of the suburbs.'
G. K. Chesterton

SUNSET OF EMPIRE

The Edwardian era is often described as the golden afternoon of the British Empire. With hindsight, it is apparent that it was very late afternoon and in thirty short years all would change forever. King Edward VII, genial and self-indulgent, reigned for ten years, and saw the world in essentially the same way as his mother Victoria. Although there were rumblings in India, the Empire was largely intact and God was in his heaven.

Roy Hattersley says that this period in English social history is *'frequently misunderstood, turbulent and the birth of modern Britain'*. Winston Churchill regarded the new king as rather vulgar, *'the embodiment of a new age in which the old standards were despised and abandoned'*. Edward believed that moral standards could be applied selectively, although there was nothing new in that. Sarcastically called Edward The Caresser by great American novelist Henry James, he saw no problem with regularly bedding his aristocratic friends' wives; on the other hand, like his mother, he regarded the Coronation as an event of spiritual significance. Hattersley again: *'God who had made Britain mighty was not going to disturb the proper order of things because of an occasional adultery'*.

C. F. G. Masterman published *The Condition of England* in 1909. He noticed a change in the character of the middle classes, which he observed was *'losing its religion and slowly discovering that it no longer believes in the existence of the God of its fathers or in life beyond the grave'*. Other commentators predicted certain disaster and the writer Rider Haggard expected an imminent apocalypse. It was the idea of rural England that perished during the reign of Edward VII. Masterman mourned its passing:

No one today would seek in the ruined villages and
dwindling population the spirit of an 'England', four fifths
of whose people have now crowded into the cities. The little
red-roofed towns and hamlets, the labourer in the field at
noontide or evening, the old English village church now
stand but as the historical survival of a once great and
splendid past. Is 'England' then to be discovered in the
feverish industrial energy of the manufacturing cities?

It is only by looking at the broad sweep of history that the
spiritual decline of England in the early years of the 20th
century becomes apparent. On the surface most indicators
seemed positive: the Empire was largely intact, although
there were growing rumblings in India; real wages of
skilled and semi-skilled workers had increased by 30 per
cent during the last quarter of the 19th century; King
Edward was a symbol of benevolent contentment, although
his morals were flexible. The horrors of two world wars
were unimagined and Edward Elgar was stamping his
genius on the national consciousness.

Edward Elgar

Elgar looked the archetypal Edwardian country gentleman.
He had the appearance - and the magnificent moustache -
of a major-general who was never happier than when
lunching at his local Conservative Club, followed by an
afternoon at a county cricket match. The breadth of his
genius made him a much loved and revered figure in
Edwardian England, especially because of his talent for
composing music which, although transcending national
boundaries, remained quintessentially 'English'. Elgar's
contemporary, Hubert Parry, who set William Blake's
Jerusalem to music, may have composed the one song which
is most associated in the public mind with this green and

pleasant land; however, Elgar's music was far more influential. It reflected a settled, ordered world-view, composed by someone whose instinct was pro Establishment; an unusual quality for an artistic genius who was a Roman Catholic and whose faith undoubtedly informed his music. The *Pomp and Circumstance March in D* was an instant success in October 1901 and from it *Land of Hope & Glory* evolved.

There was about both Edwards a smug contentment, a confidence about England's position in the world which was reflected in the royal demeanour and the sense of grandeur and certainty which pervaded the other Edward's music. All the while, religious faith continued to decline. The churches witnessed the start of the new Enlightenment with both excitement and apprehension. Because of science, men would learn to live like gods but the *'higher man'* would be led to God through science, not faith. In an age of modern miracles, the mysteries of the Church were becoming outdated.

1910 World Missionary Conference

Major Protestant denominations and missionary societies, predominantly from North America and Northern Europe, sent 1,200 representatives to Edinburgh in 1910. Before the conference convened, eight assigned commissions, each with twenty members, conducted two years of research on their assigned topic. Each commission produced a single volume report, which was distributed to all delegates before the conference.

The spirit of the conference was driven by the phrase *'The Evangelization of the World in This Generation'*. Participants at the 1910 conference testified to the strong prophetic element in the proceedings and an urgent call to unity among Protestant missionaries was made. Edinburgh 1910 was both the culmination of 19th century missions and the formal beginning of modern ecumenism. The conference led to the founding of several ecumenical projects and agencies, including the World Council of Churches in 1948.

Delegates in Edinburgh that late Edwardian summer could have little known that the following thirty-five years would see loss of life in two world wars on an unprecedented scale: the spirit of optimism so apparent in 1910 was quenched by the suffering and misery of the trenches in World War I and the annihilation of Hiroshima and Nagasaki in 1945.

Dancing into Shadow

H. G. Wells thought that Queen Victoria had *'like a great paperweight sat on men's minds and when she was removed their ideas began to blow about all over the place haphazardly.'* The summer of 1911 was especially hot and Juliet Nicholson suggests the early signs that all was not well started to surface; that as a nation, we began *'dancing into shadow'* during this first year of the new King George V's reign. Amongst the upper classes, there was a sense of urgency about the usual round of social occasions and parties: as the Countess of Fingall put it, *'we danced on the edge of an abyss.'* Juliet Nicholson: *'socialites crammed in their gaiety as intensively as the poor made their grievances heard.'*

Madame Helena Blavatsky introduced the concept of 'Theosophy' to Western consciousness, the intuitive insight into the nature of God. A cult following for Blavatsky's teachings grew in England, and the writers

James Joyce, Edwin Arnold and W. B. Yeats were among those who were influenced by her. Annie Besant, who went on to be closely associated with Mahatma Gandhi, was a President of the British Theosophical Society.

Perhaps the first echoes of the 21st century can be detected in the era after the First World War - the Twenties.

The Twenties

Noel Coward's *'talent to amuse'* manifested itself in being witty and brittle, nothing really mattering apart from *'le bon mot'*. The spirit of the Roaring Twenties was marked by a general feeling of discontinuity associated with modernity, a break with traditions. New technologies, especially automobiles, movies and radio, proliferated 'modernity' to a large part of the population. Formal decorative frills were shed in favour of practicality, in architecture as well as in daily life. At the same time, amusement, fun and lightness were cultivated in jazz and dancing, in defiance of the horrors of World War I, which remained present in people's minds. The period is also often called The Jazz Age.

War and the economic depression caused many to turn to God and others to turn away from him. Major efforts were made to spread Christianity in the 'heathen' nations and communism emerged as a force opposing Christianity. Evolution challenged Creationism. Scientific discoveries and theories flourished, causing doubt on the biblical version of events. Educational institutions promoted scientific learning based on facts, causing some to label them as *'incubators of agnosticism'*.

Beautiful Losers

The Great Gatsby, perhaps F. Scott Fitzgerald's greatest novel, encompasses themes like class, wealth and social standing; Gatsby's whole life is spent trying to attain these things. The characters live the decadent life of the roaring twenties: mindless, indulgent, and irresponsible where consequence is just an afterthought. Nick Carraway, the book's narrator: *'they were careless people, Tom and Daisy - they smashed up things and creatures and then returned to their money or their vast carelessness.'* Jay Gatsby emerges from the pages of the book as likeable - although amoral - and Daisy personifies a Twenties archetype - the 'beautiful loser'. After the horrors of war, England needed the oblivion of the jazz age, cocktails and escapism, little knowing that another terrible conflict was just around the corner.

Fitzgerald's emotional and mental deterioration from alcoholism, combined with his wife Zelda's onset of schizophrenia in 1930, after ten years of marriage, filled their lives with tragedy and despair. Zelda was in and out of mental institutions for the rest of her life. *Tender is the Night*, published in 1934, was Fitzgerald's novel set in France about a psychiatrist and his mentally ill wife; the latter modelled on Zelda. He wrote about his own emotional bankruptcy in *The Crack-Up*, a series of essays and stories. Fitzgerald is considered the definitive chronicler of the 1920s and in his work immortalized the era he dubbed the Jazz Age. Even though he was impressed with the courage, ebullience, and extravagance of the age, he was always bothered by the immorality that typically accompanied it.

The Twenties were frantic and fragmented, in a sense a reactionary decade - a reaction against Victorian ideas of morality that saw young men and women start to defy what their parents still viewed as proper behaviour for relationships between the sexes. It was a rebellious age, in which women continued the process of breaking out of older social patterns as they had begun to do during World War I. They changed their dress styles, cut their hair short, smoked in public and were not above taking a nip from a flask of prohibition whisky.

Bertrand Russell

Many lost faith during these uneasy inter-war years. As we have already seen, the certain and secure world of the 19th century had been shattered by the publication of Charles Darwin's *Origin of Species*. In the Edwardian era, G. E. Moore and Bertrand Russell emerged as eloquent opponents of the Christian beliefs which had held Victorian society together: philosophy combined with every sort of science to promote the idea that no thinking man or woman could possibly take seriously the teaching, moral or spiritual, of any church. It was not only the pressure of philosophic argument which challenged faith: some men and women, far more prosperous than before, no longer needed the comfort of a better life to come. The old miracles and mysteries of the Bible gave way to the magic of flight, wireless, radio and telegraph.

C. F. G. Masterman again: '*The nation was losing its religion and the whole apparatus of worship now seems archaic and unreal.*' George Bernard Shaw, in *Man and Superman,* scoffs at the idea of a superior being; G. K. Chesterton observed that, by the end of the Victorian era, '*atheism had become the religion of the suburbs*'.

1929 Crash

On October 24, 1929, later to be known as Black Thursday, the stock market began its downhill drop. After the first hour, the prices had gone down at an amazing speed, but many expected that prices would rise again the following day, just as before. However, prices kept dropping, and on October 29, 1929 - Black Tuesday - more than 16 million shares were sold; by the end of the day, most stocks ended below their previous value, and many stocks became totally worthless. Some people became homeless and penniless because of the stock market crash and by November 13, the prices had hit rock bottom. America had celebrated for eight years, but now everything was wasted in just a few weeks; it was a sad ending to a glorious decade.

The English Countryside

The dominant political figure in the inter-war period was Stanley Baldwin, Conservative leader and three times Prime Minister. Baldwin was the most devout Tory leader since the great Lord Salisbury, and no other Prime Minister between 1916 and 1945 could compete with him in his sincere and well advertised Christian convictions. Although the son of a Worcestershire iron-master, Baldwin was deeply attached to the English countryside, which he saw as the repository of everything best about the English character. He was admired as a trustworthy, decent and honourable man, a proponent of the consensual, wholesome, patriotic values of country life, public duty, social reconciliation and the Christian faith.

One of Baldwin's closest friends, Lord Halifax (viceroy of India 1926-31) shared his belief in the close connection between rural life and spiritual values. Here is a key thread connecting the England of today with the thirties: the English countryside. It stands for timeless values, an ordered and stable society and a more or less Christian moral consensus. Peter Ackroyd again: *'The pastoral dream of England is a calm and tranquil haven.'* In 1933-4, the BBC broadcast a series of talks on *'National Character'*, which were primarily concerned with celebrating rural England.

David Cannadine writes: *'Baldwin's belief in the regenerative power of spiritual values derived from the English countryside was genuine enough, and as such it also caught, shared and intensified a widespread inter-war mood.'* It was this concern for the beauty of the landscape, and for the moral uplift and spiritual nourishment which it provided, that lay behind such varied organisations as the National Trust, the Council for the Preservation of Rural England, the Youth Hostels Association and the Victoria History of the Counties of England. These sylvan and spiritual sentiments were shared by many men of power and influence, including Sir Edward Grey, Lord Halifax and the young R. A. Butler among politicians, Edward Elgar, Arnold Bax and Ralph Vaughan Williams amongst composers, G. M. Trevelyan, John Buchan and the young Arthur Bryant among writers and historians, and Hugh Walpole, P. G. Wodehouse and Compton Mackenzie among novelists.

Baldwin was forced to concede that during the last hundred years *'we have become largely an urban folk'* but he remained convinced that it was the countryside which embodied those *'eternal values from which we must never allow ourselves to be separated.'* Our current attachment to nostalgia is an attempt to re-create the past and stay in touch with the spiritual side of our natures.

Chapter 7

Two World Wars

'We may have won the war but it is debatable whether we
won the peace.'

Anon.

TWO WORLD WARS

The cold statistics:

- World War I: estimated deaths - 16 million, of which approx 9.7 million military and 6.8 million civilians; 21 million wounded.

- World War II: estimated deaths - 72 million, of which 25 million military and approx 47 million civilians. Of these deaths, Allied 61 million, Axis – 11 million.

The experiences of both wars led to collective trauma for all participating countries and soldiers returning home from World War I suffered greatly from the horrors they had witnessed; many returning veterans suffered from post-traumatic stress disorder, called shell shock at the time. The optimism of the 1900s was gone and those who fought in the First War became known as the Lost Generation. For the next few years, much of Europe mourned and memorials were erected in thousands of villages and towns.

It is clear from the above statistics that the human cost for the winning Allied side in World War II was far heavier than the Axis forces, but the effect of two world wars on the English *psyche* has been incalculable. The sheer horrors of conflict - especially the First World War - lacerated the English soul and, of course, we were not alone in this: other once powerful nations with substantial colonies were facing the same crisis of identity. We may have won the war but it is debatable whether we won the peace.

As with World War I, millions of young Englishmen lost their lives: this had a profound effect on their parents, who found it difficult to square the idea of a loving God with their personal bereavement. Perhaps the seeds of the Sixties detachment from Christian values was sown during the two major conflicts.

Won the War, Lost the Peace

Britain itself was left virtually bankrupt, with insolvency only averted in 1946 after the negotiation of a $3.5 billion loan from the United States, which was only fully paid off in 2006. Our resources were exhausted during six years of defending freedom. Once America entered the war in 1943, the eventual outcome was probably not in any real doubt, but it suited our transatlantic cousins for Britain to be seriously weakened. Roosevelt, in particular, couldn't abide the notion of our Empire, having been vocal in his support of Indian independence; he wanted the United States to be the premier nation, and for this to come about Britain's power would need to be correspondingly weakened.

Chapter 8

The Forties & Fifties

'By 1950, a Labour government had carried through a programme of social welfare and nationalisation seemingly impossible in 1939. But the institutions of civil society and the old ideological apparatus of the state were largely intact.'

Peter Hennessy

THE FORTIES AND FIFTIES

Welfare State

Charity is enshrined in the English soul and the welfare state is one of our greatest achievements. Our instincts for compassion and kindness towards the less fortunate steadily developed during Victorian times, although this is not to say that either the English or the Church had the monopoly on compassion. The Labour government's landslide victory in 1945 was very much about creating a new deal for '*the boys back from the front*', giving them a sense that their country had been worth fighting for and would support and care for them in peacetime; by offering them and their families jobs, homes, education, health and a standard of living of which they could be proud. The 1944 Education Act introduced compulsory free secondary education for all and the birth of the National Health Service in July 1948 was intended to care for citizens '*from the cradle to the grave*'.

With hindsight it was a blessing for Britain, as well as for its vast numbers of subjects around the world, that Winston Churchill lost the 1945 election. The old warrior was, at heart, a Victorian sentimentalist, hopelessly in love with the so called romance of empire and his antipathy to India's independence struggle, in particular, was well established: he described Gandhi as a '*crafty, half naked fakir*'. Clement Attlee, on the other hand, recognised that the British Raj was doomed, constantly reminded by Washington that the U.S. would not tolerate the continuance of Empire. Wisely, he bowed to the inevitable, and prepared for withdrawal.

India

Lord Louis Mountbatten, the last Viceroy of India, was conceited, impatient, and breathtakingly arrogant; he took to the grandeur and power of the job with unholy relish. He decided that independence would come in August 1947, on the second anniversary of the day he had accepted the surrender of the Japanese in South-East Asia. Nothing was to stand in the way of his vanity - not even the unresolved issue of Muslim demands for a separate state and the gathering storm clouds of communal violence. In a few summer weeks, British civil servants hurriedly scribbled lines across the map of the mighty subcontinent, carving East and West Pakistan out of Mother India, and sparking a bloodbath so dreadful that no one still knows exactly how many hundreds of thousands died.

The holocaust even consumed Mahatma Gandhi, who was assassinated months after independence; thus ended three hundred years of history, and one hundred and fifty years of the British Raj. King George VI would be the last British monarch to style himself Emperor of India. True, 'Dickie' Mountbatten was put under pressure by his political masters in Whitehall to hasten the dismantling of the *'jewel in the crown'*, but our removal from the sub-continent with such indecent haste is a stain on us as a nation. Losing such a significant chunk of Empire started to significantly change our perception of ourselves: the old colonial certainties were fracturing and the anxieties of the Cold War beckoned.

Although Britain had shed responsibility for India in 1947, she still saw herself as a major global power and her expenditure on defence in 1951 accounted for a whopping 20 per cent of total public expenditure or 7.6 per cent of GDP. The Second World War had left the nation on it uppers financially and it simply did not have the cash to fund Clement Attlee and his senior ministers' appetite for world-class status. The true state of the country's finances was largely kept secret from the nation, because it was deemed crucial to engender a 'feelgood' factor. International historian Paul Kennedy puts it thus: *'It is very difficult psychologically to be in the first.... or second generation of the decision makers who confront relative decline and feel that they have to do something about it. And it seems perfectly natural, knowing how human beings behave, that they tend to deny it and say "Well look, all it needs is a patch-up job or a little bit of change here, not a major transformation".'*

Cold War

Although we didn't have the money, back in 1952 it was taken for granted that we still had to be perceived as a major international power. The Cold War brought fear, living in the shadow of the Bomb, and old certainties gave way to anxiety and insecurity. Because the expression 'Cold War' is nowadays hardly ever used, it is important to remember that in the early fifties Russia and communism were seen as major threats. Churchill coined the phrase 'Iron Curtain' and Foreign Secretary Anthony Eden explained to Cabinet:

> *Reducing the value of the UK as a partner and ally would undermine the cohesion of the Commonwealth and the special relationship with the Unites States and its European partners and other allies. Their attitude towards us will depend largely on our status as a World Power and upon their belief that we are ready and willing to support them.*

Although for us in the 21st century this notion of prestige is out-dated, we have to remember that here was a country which had recently defeated the mighty German Reich and was desperate to retain its status as a world power. It is not overstating the case to say that our economic well-being was sacrificed on the altar of prestige. The English have always excelled at pomp and circumstance and weren't about to give these up without a fight. Andrew Shonfield, an economist, wrote at the time:

> *The root of Britain's economic troubles are the political objectives of a great power... the central failure of post-war Britain is inadequate investment, crippled by political choices which allowed the maintenance of a big defence budget and the sustenance of a reserve currency to produce one balance of payments crisis after another.*

England's sense of self-esteem, so bound up in our imperial past, was taking a battering. Because the old order was unravelling fast, it was easier for the old morality to unwind: this created the conditions in the sixties where the pace of social change would have been unthinkable just ten years previously.

Age of Austerity

Attlee's government took office in a world changing at bewildering speed. The war had forged new alliances, the greatest and most nebulous of which was the United Nations. The USA and the USSR were undisputed superpowers; Britain and France deluded themselves that they were too. In the Far East, the embers of nationalism had been stirred into flame by the brutal advance and subsequent stubborn retreat of Japan. Britain's ignominious surrender of Singapore in 1941 had sent a clear signal to Asia that the days of European imperialism were numbered.

There was another colonial retreat, in a way just as disgraceful, on the extreme West of Asia. For just over a quarter of a century British administrators had tried, and on the whole failed, to make sense of their League of Nations (later United Nations) mandate to rule Palestine. They tried partition, appeasement, manipulation and plain coercion. Nothing helped assuage the bloody friction between the rising tide of Jewish immigrants and the native Palestinians. The end of the Second World War brought new waves of refugees from Nazi tyranny to the shores of the Holy Land, and the conflict became more unholy than ever. Washington was adamant that nothing should stand in the way of the establishment of Israel and when the mandate finally dribbled into the sands of history in May 1948, the new state was born, fighting for its life.

Special Relationship

Elsewhere, of course, Britain's imperial might remained intact. The Union flag still flew over huge tracts of Africa, whole archipelagos in the Caribbean and Pacific, jewels of Asia like Singapore and Hong Kong. But there was another much greater reality: British adherence to, and even dependence on, the patronage of the United States. We tagged along with Washington in the occupation of Germany and the establishment of Nato; we acquiesced in the new division of Europe between East and West; we willingly did our bit in the great airlift which saved West Berlin from the Soviet blockade of the late 1940s, and we sent our troops to South Korea to fight for the United Nations - under U.S. direction - against China and the North. At the insistence of Attlee and the Labour right, we developed our very own nuclear weapons and insisted that they kept us independent. In reality, the North Atlantic connection was the only one which ultimately mattered.

It is tempting to think of the Attlee years as an anti-climax. After the clamour of victory, the peace was a drab disappointment. And after all the fervent promises of a new dawn, British life remained to a large extent grey and grim. At times, food restrictions were even tighter than during the war - bread was rationed for the first time. Class enmities flourished; social and economic inequalities remained palpable. Here and there were little pockets of a new prosperity: television broadcasts were resumed, the first Morris Minors appeared, and British designers were working on the world's first commercial jet, the De Havilland Comet. But of that great universal prosperity which seemed to glow from the 1945 manifestos, there was little sign.

We are a better people for having shed colonialism, because it has helped us to appreciate the position of the underdog, playing to our national strengths of compassion and tolerance. By whose authority did we subjugate the mighty nation of India? Back in the 19th century the prevailing belief was that we had received a specific mandate from the Almighty. '*Ask any man what nationality he would prefer to be, and ninety nine out of a hundred will tell you that they would prefer to be* an *Englishman*' - Cecil Rhodes. I repeat this quotation here, because if the loss of Empire has done nothing more than purge us of Rhodes' overweening arrogance, it has been worthwhile.

Austerity

The period between the end of the war and the late 1950s is often referred to as the 'age of austerity'. I still remember as a very young child my mother using ration books in a local grocer's store. Although the rise of the welfare state was accompanied by full employment, rationing continued until the mid-1950s. The mood of the country was dour, unexciting and intensely conservative and even the rhetoric of Nye Bevan's welfare state resonated with Victorian religious philanthropy, with its talk of educating the working-class girl and preventing juvenile delinquency.

Female liberation was an idea that had little currency in those days. The film *Brief Encounter* (1945), written by Noel Coward, explores a woman's claustrophobic fear of public discovery of her extra-marital love affair. She worries that people can *'read my secret thoughts'* and blushes when a vicar stares at her on a train. Shot in black and white, the film is so English, all buttoned up, with clipped sentences; and in the end the woman (Celia Johnson) terminates the affair, realising the 'duty' of her role as wife and mother and her unbearable guilt at this forbidden tryst.

During the war, the traditional female role had changed, often because it had to: women were often employed in factories to assist in the war effort. It is also widely acknowledged - although not much discussed - that sexual morality loosened since often young couples had no certainty that they would meet again. But peacetime brought with it a return to the traditional values of family, home and piety. Evelyn Home, writing in Woman magazine in 1951, puts it thus... *'most women, once they have a family, are more contented and doing better work in the home than they could find outside it.'* As late as 1961, a columnist in Woman's Own advised:

> *You can't have deep and safe happiness in a marriage and the exciting independence of a career as well. It isn't fair on your husband. I believe any man would tell you he would rather his wife stayed at home and looked after his children, and was waiting for him with a decent meal and a sympathetic ear when he got home from work.*

Church Revival

Interestingly, the late 1940s and 1950s witnessed the greatest church growth that Britain had experienced since the mid-19th century. Sociologists and social historians have never come to terms with the growth of institutional religion during these times. Virtually all mainline Protestant churches experienced a surge in growth between 1955 and 1959. The Billy Graham crusades of 1954-56 drew mass audiences in football stadia, military barracks and evening congregations of tens of thousands in large indoor arenas. These major crusades spawned hundreds of smaller *Come Back to God* rallies and meetings: as a ten year old in 1958 I attended one such event on a field near my home in Perivale, West London.

C. S. Lewis

In addition to his career as an English professor and author of fiction, Lewis is regarded by many as one of the most influential Christian apologists of his time. In the Fifties and Sixties, The Oxford Don seemed almost a lone Christian voice in the marketplace, a mainstream author whose books had a wide appeal. There was so much sheer common-sense in his approach to faith.

Lewis was committed to presenting a reasonable case for the truth of Christianity. *Mere Christianity*, *The Problem of Pain*, and *Miracles* were all concerned, to one degree or another, with refuting popular objections to Christianity. Lewis also wrote an autobiography titled *Surprised by Joy*, which placed special emphasis on his own conversion; the title of the book came from the first line of a poem by William Wordsworth. From *Mere Christianity:*

The great difficulty is to get modern audiences to realise that you are preaching Christianity solely and simply because you happen to think it true; they always suppose you are preaching it because you think it good for society or something of that sort.

In a much cited passage in the book *Mere Christianity*, Lewis challenged the increasingly popular view that Jesus, although a great moral teacher, was not God. He argued that Jesus made several implicit claims to divinity, which would logically exclude this:

The really foolish thing that people often say about Jesus is: I'm ready to accept Jesus as a great moral teacher, but I don't accept his claim to be God. That is the one thing we must not say. A man who was merely a man and said the sort of things Jesus said would not be a great moral teacher. He would either be a lunatic − on the level with the man who says he is a poached egg − or else he would be the Devil of Hell. You must make your choice. Either this man was, and is, the Son of God, or else a madman or something worse, but let us not come with any patronising nonsense about his being a great human teacher. He has not left that open to us. He did not intend to.

There is a real need for Christian apologists of Lewis' stature today: men and women able to explain biblical truth in an accessible way without recourse to religious jargon, using allegory as in the *Chronicles of Narnia*. World class figures like Lewis' close friend J. R. R. Tolkien, who taught great truths in *Lord of The Rings*, individuals whose 'centre of gravity' is in the mainstream, not in the Church.

Chapter 9

The Sixties

'It only took us forty years to forsake Christianity, compared to the thousand or so years of practising it.'

Calum Brown

THE SIXTIES

The sixties polarized the English. Pessimists saw the decade as the period when everything began to fall apart, when the nation undid itself, when the sniggering of the satirists and the misguided reforms of liberalism tore the fabric of morals and social cohesion. The optimists viewed the same changes as the start of freedom. As one who grew up during this time there is little doubt that the triple whammy of the Abortion Act, contraceptive pill and decriminalisation of homosexuality dealt a fatal blow to the consensual Christian morality.

The sixties was primarily a watershed of ideas: it was an intense period when the mental landscape of the nation changed - forever. A different spirit was on the wind, blowing away the shared Christian consensus, ushering in a revolution of ideas. Old constraints were cast off, new paradigms of behaviour readily accepted. It was as if the stern housemistress had gone on a long holiday and the boys could now do as they pleased. Ex Prime Minister Tony Blair's attack on the sixties follows a long-established pattern of citing the era of flower power, drugs and rock'n'roll as the cause of society's moral disintegration.

Satire

Of course, satire has been around for a very long time: the Victorians had *Punch* magazine, and in 1961 *Private Eye* was launched. Four very clever graduates, two (Jonathan Miller and Peter Cook) from Cambridge and two (Alan Bennett and Dudley Moore) from Oxford, wrote and presented the satirical revue *Beyond The Fringe* at the

Edinburgh Festival. So popular was this show that it went on to sell out in London's West End and successfully transferred to Broadway. It kick-started the sixties satire boom almost single-handedly and led to numerous imitations including one, *Behind the Fridge*, from two of the original cast.

The revue was widely considered to be ahead of its time, both in its unapologetic willingness to debunk figures of authority, and by virtue of its inherent surrealism. Humiliation of authority was something only previously delved into in *The Goon Show* and, arguably, *Hancock's Half Hour*, with such parliamentarians as Sir Winston Churchill and Harold Macmillan coming under special scrutiny. Macmillan, according to Cook, was not particularly fond of the slurred caricature and charade of senile forgetfulness (marked by a failure to coherently pronounce 'Conservative Party') portrayed in Cook's impersonation.

It is no accident that Peter Cook's Establishment Club and the TV programme *That Was The Week That Was* were launched in the sixties. Given the success of *TW3*, as the programme became known, which brought in an average of three million viewers, satire came to rely heavily on politics as a crutch. Though it aimed to remain apolitical, there was no doubt that the members of the satire club were mainly to the left of centre (at least for show; a few were actually Tories), and therefore relished the idea of attacking the reigning Conservatives. However, even Prime Minister Macmillan, a constant source of attack on *TW3* once wrote to the Post Master General, claiming: *'I hope you will not, repeat not, take any action against That Was The Week That Was without consulting me. It is a good thing to be laughed over - it is better than to be ignored.'*

All You Need is Love

The Vietnam War provoked a widespread sense of demoralisation that encouraged a major re-evaluation of the Western way of life. Many observers drew attention to the fact that in the 1960s the moral balance between the West and the Third World appeared to favour the latter. According to the 'end-of-ideology' sociologist Seymour Lipset, '*the extent to which major segments of the intellectual and bureaucratic elites have lost faith in the moral superiority of Western democracy generally and of the United States in particular was a source of real concern.*'

The Beatles' *Sergeant Pepper's Lonely Hearts Club Band*, released in 1966, was a cultural milestone, reflecting the new ideas and values sweeping in to our shores. Tinged with drug references but held together, as always, by Lennon and McCartney's genius for melody, the LP excited a generation to a world of new possibilities: the old order had been swept away. Radio Caroline and the pirate ships off the North Sea, dramatised in Richard Curtis' *The Boat that Rocked* further legitimated youth culture and Caroline also promoted the founder's new concept of 'LA' (Loving Awareness), a Far Eastern inspired philosophy of love and peace. In the film, Kenneth Branagh plays the Minister tasked with outlawing pirate radio and is the obvious buttoned-up, repressed Establishment figure intent on spoiling the youngsters' fun.

There is no doubt that England - and especially London - in the mid sixties was a very exciting place to be. There was a sense that anything was possible and a renewed hope that human beings - through love and flower power - could save the planet. The Church all of a sudden looked very old-fashioned and irrelevant and feverish attempts were made to appear 'with it' by wheeling on Cliff Richard at evangelistic rallies.

Whirlwind of Change

There is a view - widely held by sociologists - that Christianity in England declined gradually over the last two hundred years. I disagree: instead, the middle years of the sixties brought about a whirlwind of abrupt change in moral and spiritual attitudes - with profound and irreversible consequences. There was a sea change in the realm of ideas and it was as if permission had at last been granted for the young to look beyond the faith of their fathers.

Personal Christian identity broke down suddenly in the 'swinging sixties' when new media, new gender roles and the moral revolution dramatically ended the English's conception that they lived Christian lives. What began in the sixties was the death of the culture which previously conferred Christian identity upon the English. Calum Brown:

> *Whereas previously, men and women were able to draw upon a Christian-centred culture to find guidance about how they should behave, and how they should think about their lives, from the 1960s a suspicion of creeds arose that quickly took the form of a rejection of Christian tradition and all formulaic constructions of the individual. If a core reality survives for Britons, it is certainly no longer Christian. It only took us forty years to forsake Christianity, compared to the thousand or so years of practicing it.*
>
> *The generation that grew up in the sixties was more dissimilar to the generation of its parents than in any previous century. The moral metamorphosis directly affected the churches' domain: the decline of marriage, the rise of divorce and remarriage, the rise of cohabitation in place of marriage... decreasing stigmatisation of illegitimacy, homosexuality and sexual licence, the*

growing recourse to birth control and abortion, and the irresistible social pressures for government liberalisation of restrictions on drinking, Sunday closing and recreation.

Brown also suggests that what was different in the mid sixties was the reaction of women and that in the Christian culture women had played a crucial role in taming men and bringing them into the church. In novels and magazines the women were always the domestic saints, the men the potential prodigals. In the sixties women were no longer prepared to be the guardians of the Christian home, and this rejection of pious femininity destroyed the *'evangelical narrative'*. With this rejection came a massive exodus from the church.

Roy Jenkins

Roy Jenkins, Labour politician and one of the founding fathers of the SDP in the early eighties, was a progressive, liberally minded, heavyweight politician. He was influenced by the morally flexible ideas sweeping Europe in the era of the Beatles. He was accused of being 'trendy' but he was no political lightweight: Edward Heath, the former Tory Prime Minister, said *'Roy Jenkins had a thorough intellectual grasp of this country and its problems, and of all world affairs.'*

Permissive Society

Jenkins earned himself the epithet *'architect of the permissive society'* in the press. During his time as Home Secretary, David Steel's Abortion Act made it to the statute book, homosexuality was de-criminalised, theatre censorship was abolished, the contraceptive pill superseded the condom and divorce was made much easier. Jenkins saw himself as a libertarian, a defender of individual rights against the state. In his Guardian obituary of Lord Jenkins, David Marquand listed four 'achievements' of his hero on which, to him, *'the verdict of history seems plain'*. As Home Secretary, *'Jenkins did more than any other person to make Britain a more civilised country to live in'*. Neil Clark of *The Telegraph* challenges this view:

> Jenkins was of course convinced that the 'permissive society' was the 'civilised society'. In this, he - alas - got it all terribly wrong. What underpins civilised society is not permissiveness, but self-restraint, a phrase detested by libertines of both Left and Right. What Jenkins failed to see was how the freedoms he espoused would lead to the degeneration of British society and the selfish, me-first libertinism of today.

> He also embarked on the most radical programme of penal reform since the Second World War. His Criminal Justice Act of 1967 said very little about the victims of crime, but plenty about the perpetrators. In two years, Jenkins had succeeded in transforming the criminal justice system from one whose raison d'etre had been to deter wrong-doing to one designed to be as 'civilised' as possible to the criminal.

> Jenkins was never a socialist, but in my view he was not much of a liberal either. Classical liberalism always understood that liberal freedom is dependent on moral self-restraint. Without it, freedom becomes licence - which itself is a threat to freedom, as it acknowledges no obligation to others. Before the Jenkins-sponsored social reforms made their impact, Britain was a country famous for the self-restraint of its people. 'Letting it all

hang out', extreme displays of emotion, and shouting and swearing in the street were all considered unacceptable. For Jenkins, the taboos that existed in 1950s Britain were intolerable. But the net result was a society remarkable for its civility.

More than thirty-five years on, the damaging impact of Jenkins's reforms on the society we live in is all too clear to see. One marriage in three now ends in divorce. Almost 40 per cent of children are now born out of wedlock, the highest figure in Europe. The policy of early release of prisoners has had a catastrophic effect on the safety of the general public: 14 per cent of violent criminals freed early are convicted of fresh violence within two years of their release.

Dividing his time between the palaces of Westminster, the delightful Oxfordshire village of East Hendred and the high table of the Oxford colleges, Jenkins did not, of course, see too much of the social debris that his 'civilising' reforms had caused. Had he seen at first hand what the 'permissive society' amounts to in practice on a 'sink' council estate, he might have modified his views.

Abortion Act

Between six to seven million abortions have been performed since the Abortion Act, introduced in 1967. The Act was introduced by David Steel MP primarily to stop back street abortions but in 1969, the first full year that abortion figures were available, the number of children legally killed by abortion was 54,819, rising to 195,300 in 2008. As with many reforms, the Act had precisely the opposite effect to that intended.

The Pill

This was, on the face of it, a very sensible idea. The contraceptive pill was originally inextricably linked to the phrase 'family planning', intended for use by the married woman who wanted a more convenient method of birth control than the coil or condom. As with so many sixties' innovations, the pill had unintended consequences. Sociologists surveyed the sexual attitudes and practices of unmarried women and found major changes in sexual behaviour: instead of the rigmarole of the condom which places the onus for contraception on the careless, passionate male, the pill, a combination of an estrogen (oestrogen) and a progestin (progestogen), could be popped into the handbag by the more responsible female and thus used to neutralise the results of last night's hanky-panky. On University and Polytechnic campuses across the land, the availability of the pill changed sexual behaviour, literally overnight.

Lords of Misrule

Mirroring the loosening of morality in public life, there grew up a generation in the sixties who rejected the shared Christian mindset inherited from previous generations. This manifested itself in the 'free love' of the hippy rock festivals like Woodstock and films like *Alfie* starring Michael Caine, a role reprised more recently by Jude Law. Alfie is a lovable rogue whose main aim in life is to bed as many women as possible, with scant regard for them as human beings; the film maker casts him as hero and gives a tacit nod to his amoral behaviour. The swinging sixties are seen as an innocent, carefree time and there is little doubt that after the austerity of the fifties, England badly needed some fun. We certainly did not want to return to the rigid, class-ridden England of the inter-war years.

George Melly, a man with little talent but a huge capacity for dissolution, is in many ways a typical sixties Englishman. Louche, with very flexible morals and lifestyle, he built a career on a good knowledge of jazz, a modest voice and relentlessly 'daring' clothes. Near to death, wild-eyed and sad, he appeared on TV and was applauded for the 'freedom' which had characterized his life. He looked old - and very afraid. A. N. Wilson: *'He was depressing, not because he was immoral, but second-rate and made gallant efforts to show off and shock people until he died.'* John Mortimer was a playwright, author and barrister, an old Harrovian whose pudgy expression and dribbling lips seemed like an embodiment of moral as well as physical dilapidation. Both Melly and Mortimer were especially unattractive representatives of the permissive society.

Mary Whitehouse

After raising her children and returning to teaching, Mary Whitehouse became responsible for sex education at Madeley Modern School in Shropshire in the early 1960s. At this time, shocked at the response of her pupils to moral issues, she became concerned about what she and many others perceived as declining moral standards in the British media, especially in the BBC. In the 1960s, she set up the *National Viewers and Listeners Association*. Her support base included social conservatives and Christians and among her staunchest allies was the Catholic Labour peer Lord Longford, a campaigner against pornography.

She was a leading figure in the *Nationwide Festival of Light* of 1971, which protested against the commercial exploitation of sex and violence in Britain.

By the 1980s, Mary Whitehouse had found an ally in the Conservative government, particularly in Margaret Thatcher herself. Senior television executives commented that her views were not disregarded lightly, particularly if she had the ear of the Prime Minister. It has been claimed though, that the market orientation of the Thatcher government actually prejudiced that government against Whitehouse in private.

Writing in the *Dictionary of National Biography*, the philosopher Mary Warnock comments, *'Even if her campaigning did not succeed in "cleaning up TV", still less in making it more fit to watch in other ways, she was of serious intent, and was an influence for good at a crucial stage in the development both of the BBC and of ITV. She was not, as the BBC seemed officially to proclaim, a mere figure of fun.'*

Chapter 10

Margaret Thatcher
& the Demise of the Tories

'I thought I was running for leadership of the Conservative party, not some demented Marxist sect.'

Douglas Hurd

MARGARET THATCHER
and the Demise of the Tories

Margaret Hilda Roberts was born on 13 October 1925 in Grantham, Lincolnshire, daughter of a grocer. She went to Oxford University and then became a research chemist, re-training to become a barrister in 1954. In 1951, she married a wealthy businessman, Denis Thatcher, with whom she had two children: the surprisingly normal Carole and the incredibly obnoxious Mark. Margaret Thatcher was Britain's first female Prime Minister and served three consecutive terms in office. She is one of the dominant political figures of 20th century Britain, and Thatcherism continues to have a huge influence.

Mrs Thatcher became Conservative Member of Parliament for Finchley, North London in 1959, serving as its MP until 1992. Her first parliamentary post was junior minister for pensions in Harold Macmillan's government and from 1964 to 1970, when Labour were in power, she served in a number of positions in Edward Heath's shadow cabinet. Heath became Prime Minister in 1970 and Thatcher was appointed Secretary for Education. After the Conservatives were defeated in 1974, Thatcher challenged Heath for the leadership of the party and, to the surprise of many, won. In the 1979 general election, the Conservatives came to power and Thatcher became Prime Minister.

An advocate of privatisation of state-owned industries and utilities, reform of the trade unions, the lowering of taxes and reduced social expenditure across the board, Thatcher's policies succeeded in reducing inflation, but unemployment dramatically increased. She acknowledges that Gladstone influenced her fiscal policies. Victory in the

Falklands War in 1982 and a divided opposition helped Thatcher win a landslide victory in the 1983 general election. In 1984, she narrowly escaped death when the IRA planted a bomb at the Conservative Party Conference in Brighton.

In foreign affairs, Thatcher cultivated a close political and personal relationship with U.S. president Ronald Reagan, based on a common mistrust of communism, combined with free market economic ideology. Thatcher was nicknamed the 'Iron Lady' by the Soviets and warmly welcomed the rise of reformist Soviet leader Mikhail Gorbachev. In the 1987 general election, Thatcher won an unprecedented third term in office. But controversial policies, including the poll tax and her opposition to any closer integration with Europe, produced divisions within the Conservative Party which led to a leadership challenge. In November 1990, she had to be surgically removed from the Tory leadership and was succeeded as party leader and Prime Minister by John Major.

History will not be kind to Margaret Thatcher. Quentin Letts says that, although Thatcher's record was commendable in many respects, her ruthless response to the miners' strike did *'lasting damage to our country'*. True, the miners were led by a politically suicidal maniac -Arthur Scargill -who could not be allowed to succeed, but there was something ugly and vengeful in the way she prosecuted the war. The miners themselves were a remarkable body of men who did tough jobs with great stoicism and humour. The subsequent closure of nearly all of Britain's coal mines makes it hard to deny that the government intended, all along, to wreck the country's coal industry. Never trust a man with a comb-over.

Regardless of one's political affiliation, there was always something vaguely reassuring about the Tories just being there during those years. As familiar as HP sauce and the Daily Telegraph, the Tories were the 'National Trust' of politics, preserving and reinforcing the familiar in public life. The breakdown of the old class system in the sixties was mirrored in the way the conservatives went about choosing their leaders: the last of the old guard of 'patrician' Tory leaders, Sir Alec Douglas Home, was clearly out of step with the mood of the country in 1963-64. Followed by Edward Heath, a carpenter's son from Broadstairs, Kent, and Margaret Thatcher, a grocer's daughter from Lincolnshire- the party pulled John Major out of the hat in 1990.

Geoffrey Wheatcroft: *'Before now the Tories had done improbable things and chosen unlikely leaders, but none quite as unlikely as this. Heath in 1965 and Thatcher in 1975 had been surprising; Major was astonishing.'* Robert Musil described him as *'a man without qualities'* and Kitty Muggeridge, Malcolm's wife, stated that he had *'risen without trace'*. It is clear that in choosing Major rather than the obvious successor to Maggie, Douglas Hurd, the Conservatives betrayed an unmistakable loss of nerve on the part of those who for so long had ruled England. Hurd was the 'Establishment' candidate - but Macmillan before him had been cruelly lampooned by Peter Cook back in the early sixties, when the Establishment first came under attack from the rising generation of satirists.

So uncomfortable had the Tories become with their upper class, aristocratic connections that Douglas Hurd was forced to almost disown his past. Educated at Eton and Trinity College, Cambridge, he was the son of Lord Hurd, a landowning farmer and journalist. The normally unflappable politician became almost distraught ... *'I was brought up on a farm. I don't know how we got into all this. This is inverted snobbery. I thought I was running for leadership of the*

Conservative party, not some demented Marxist sect.' It is significant that in a few short years the *'natural party of government'* became detached from its class roots, mirroring a wider societal loosening of class boundaries.

Sleaze

After a decade of the stridency and anger of Mrs Thatcher, the Tories wanted a quiet life - another reason for choosing John Major. Political journalist Alan Watkins compared the parliamentary conservative party under Major with a *'chap whose wife has left home and who could now spend the day loafing around in a dressing gown, drinking from a mug instead of a cup and neglecting to shave.'*

Even before Thatcher's demise the Tories had often looked shabby or shady, but they had at least retained some credit for economic competence. David Mellor was National Heritage Secretary - or *'Minister of Fun'*, as the tabloids called him. In the summer of 1992 he became a national laughing stock because of revelations of extramarital sex, possibly whilst in Chelsea football club kit. Universally loathed, Major hung on to him far too long and the Government was damaged. Alan Clark - Trade Minister between 1986 and 1989 - landed in hot water in the Matrix Churchill affair; Jonathan Aitken landed in prison for perjury, although he was subsequently rehabilitated as an evangelical Christian.

At the 1993 Conservative Party Conference, Major began the *'Back to Basics'* campaign, which he intended to be about the economy, education, policing, and other such issues, but it was interpreted by many (including Conservative cabinet ministers) as an attempt to revert to the moral and family values that the Conservative Party were often associated with. *'Back to Basics'*, however, became synonymous with scandal, often exposed by tabloid newspapers such as *The Sun*. The wife of the Earl of Caithness committed suicide amongst rumours of the Earl committing adultery; David Ashby was 'outed' by his wife after sleeping with men. A string of other Conservative MPs, including Alan Amos, Tim Yeo and Michael Brown, were involved in sexual scandals.

Other debilitating incidents included 'Cash for Questions', in which first Graham Riddick, and David Tredinnick accepted money to ask questions in the House of Commons in a newspaper 'sting', and later Tim Smith and Neil Hamilton were found to have received money from Mohamed Al Fayed, also to ask questions in the House. Later, David Willetts resigned as Paymaster General after he was accused of rigging evidence to do with 'Cash for Questions'. Jonathan Aitken's Parliamentary Aide was Stephen Milligan, who died a spectacularly bizarre auto-erotic death.

Shirt Tucked into Underpants

One of John Major's worst mistakes must surely be his espousal of Jeffrey Archer, one of the most unprincipled men ever to hold high office. When asked whether Archer was fit to be an MP, a close colleague said *'he should be in a remand home.'* His life was a web of fraud and fantasy, but in 1992 Major made him Lord Archer of Weston-super-Mare; like Aitken before him, Archer brought a libel action on perjured evidence and was to write his prison memoirs. Major's elevation of Archer epitomised all that was wrong with the Tories. Second only to his choice of Jeffrey Archer was his choice of the kiss and tell dragon Edwina Currie as his bedfellow: she revealed that he tucked his shirt tails into his underpants and this may have been the final nail in the coffin.

During his leadership of the Conservative Party, Major was portrayed as honest ('Honest John') but was unable to rein in the philandering and bickering within his party. Major's appearance was noted in its greyness, his prodigious philtrum, and large glasses, all of which were exaggerated in caricatures. In TV's *Spitting Image*, Major's puppet was changed from a circus performer to that of a grey man who ate dinner with his wife in silence, occasionally saying *'nice peas, dear'*. He was often mocked for his nostalgic evocation of what sounded like the lost England of the 1950s: *'Fifty years on from now, Britain will still be the country of long shadows on cricket grounds, warm beer, invincible green suburbs, dog lovers and pools fillers.'*

Chapter 11

Blair & Brown

'Whatever that young man is, he is not a Socialist.'
Anonymous Labour Grandee on Tony Blair

BLAIR AND BROWN

Anthony Charles Lynton Blair (born 6 May 1953) served as Prime Minister from 2 May 1997 to 27 June 2007. He was elected Leader of the Labour Party in the leadership election of July 1994, following the sudden death of his predecessor, the genial and popular John Smith. Blair's political persona has been described as one of charisma and charm, and he is one of Britain's most internationally recognised statesmen. Blair was the Labour Party's longest-serving Prime Minister and the only leader to have taken the party to three consecutive general election victories, two of them landslides.

He was influenced by fellow student and Anglican priest Peter Thomson, who awakened within Blair a religious faith and, perhaps nominally, left wing politics. Whilst at Oxford, his mother Hazel died of cancer, which greatly affected him. After graduating from Oxford in 1976, Blair became a member of Lincoln's Inn, enrolled as a pupil barrister and met his future wife, Cherie Booth. He converted to Catholicism soon after stepping down as Prime Minister in 2008 in favour of Gordon Brown. Interviewed by Michael Parkinson on ITV1 in March 2006, Blair referred to the role of his Christian faith in his decision to go to war in Iraq, stating that he had prayed about the issue, and saying that God would judge him for his decision: *'I think if you have faith about these things, you realise that judgment is made by other people... and if you believe in God, it's made by God as well.'*

Blair raised taxes (but did not increase income tax for high earners); introduced a minimum wage and some new employment rights (while keeping Margaret Thatcher's trade union legislation); introduced significant constitutional reforms; promoted new rights for gay people in the Civil Partnership Act 2004; and signed treaties integrating Britain more closely with the EU. He introduced substantial market-based reforms in the education and health sectors; introduced student tuition fees; sought to reduce certain categories of welfare payments, and introduced tough anti-terrorism and identity card legislation.

Young Idealist

It is his personal tragedy, as well as the tragedy of the Labour Party, that the ambitious idealist was transformed into a surprisingly authoritarian politician. While researching a history of the Parliamentary Labour Party since 1906, journalist Robert Taylor came across an extraordinary, 22 page, handwritten letter from the 29 year old Blair to the then Labour leader, Michael Foot. Found among the Foot papers in the Labour Party archive in Manchester, the letter was composed at his chambers, 1 Harcourt Buildings in the Temple, London. It is dated 28 July 1982, at a time when the breakaway Social Democrats under the leadership of Roy Jenkins, in alliance with the Liberals, threatened Labour's prime position on the centre left of British politics.

As a young man just entering politics, it is clear that Blair had a credible vision for the British left. Foot never disguised his admiration for the young and ambitious barrister after campaigning for Blair during the Beaconsfield by-election. His warm feelings towards him were reciprocated, as Blair's letter reveals. It begins: *'Dear Michael, Read this in a quiet moment if you have any nowadays. And don't, for goodness' sake, bother to reply! I was very hesitant in writing: you might consider it either an impertinence or sycophancy. It isn't meant to be either.'* Blair had just finished reading Foot's 1980 collection of biographical essays on writers and politicians, *Debts of Honour.* He writes:

> *There was hope and vigour and something irrepressibly optimistic that struck a deep chord in me. It is so abundantly plain to me when I read D of H that there is a treasure trove of ideas that I never imagined existed. We need to recover the searching radicalism of these people. Like many middle class people I came to Socialism through Marxism. The trouble with Marxism is that it is fine if you make it your political servant but terrible if it becomes your political master; ultimately it was stifling because it sought to embrace in its philosophy every facet of existence. It is impossible to understand the 20-40 age group in today's Labour Party without understanding the pervasiveness of Marxist teaching. For me at university, left-wing politics was Marx and the liberal tradition was either scorned or analysed only in terms of its influence on Marx.*

The letter brings back not only a nostalgic reminder of that unlamented lost world of Labour, but why so many people found Tony Blair so attractive, electing him their leader in 1994. There is a strangely adolescent feeling to what he writes, suggesting a man who wants desperately to impress his leader. He did not shy away from flattery or loyalty to a man who was to lead the Labour Party to one of its worst election defeats less than 12 months later, fighting on a manifesto that came to be known as *'the longest suicide note in history'.*

Tony Blair addressed the National Prayer Breakfast in Washington DC in 2009 as the guest of President Obama. Here are some highlights:

> *Today, religion is under attack from without and from within. From within, it is corroded by extremists who use*

their faith as a means of excluding the other. I am what I am in opposition to you. If you do not believe as I believe, you are a lesser human being.

From without, religious faith is assailed by an increasingly aggressive secularism, which derides faith as contrary to reason and defines faith by conflict. Thus do the extreme believers and the aggressive non-believers come together in unholy alliance.

And yet, faith will not be so easily cast. For billions of people, faith motivates, galvanises, compels and inspires, not to exclude but to embrace; not to provoke conflict but to try to do good. This is faith in action. You can see it in countless local communities where those from churches, mosques, synagogues and temples, tend the sick, care for the afflicted, work long hours in bad conditions to bring hope to the despairing and salvation to the lost. You can see it in the arousing of the world's conscience to the plight of Africa.

The Foundation which bears my name is dedicated to achieving understanding, action and reconciliation between the different faiths for the common good. It is not about the faith that looks inward; but the faith that resolutely turns us towards each other. While here on earth, we need to make a vital decision... whether to be mere spectators, or movers and shakers for the Kingdom of God... whether to stay among the curious, or take up a cross. And this means: no standing on the sidelines ...

With the baton being handed from Blair to Brown, in Part Three we will look at the sort of England that Brown inherited. As a nation, we are clearly more prosperous than we were fifty years ago; there have been tremendous advances in health care; our infrastructure is sound and efficient; we have incredible consumer choice. But we are not at ease with ourselves. As Jeremy Paxman says *'The belief that something has rotted in England is widely held: a people cannot spend decades being told their civilisation is in decline and not be affected by it.'*

Fingers in the Till

The MPs' Expenses Scandal in 2009, initiated by the Daily Telegraph's publishing of MPs' expenses claims, has shaken our faith in politicians and the institution of democracy itself. We know that Home Secretary Jacqui Smith's husband charged the taxpayer for viewing pornography; Conservative MP and Eurosceptic Bill Cash claimed £1200 per month in rent paid to his daughter on her Notting Hill flat, despite already owning an empty flat in Pimlico, a short walk from the Commons. Elliot Morley, the former minister was suspended by the Labour Party after he claimed for a mortgage that had been paid off; Margaret Moran claimed more than £20,000 to treat dry rot in a house 100 miles from her constituency.

Professor Colin Rallings, director of Plymouth University's Election Data Centre, said after analysing the fallout from The Daily Telegraph's expenses investigation: *'By the time the British public has voted at the next general election, as many as 325 MPs – more than half the entire House of Commons – will have either quit or lost their seats in the biggest parliamentary upheaval since the Civil War.'* It was clear during the election campaign in May 2010 that the question of MPs' expenses was still a hot potato and that faith in politicians was at an all time low.

Part 3

England Present

Chapter 12

Agog with Indifference

'When you gonna wake up, when you gonna wake up
When you gonna wake up strengthen the things that remain?'
Bob Dylan

AGOG WITH INDIFFERENCE

When you gonna wake up, when you gonna wake up
When you gonna wake up   strengthen the things that
  remain?

These lines, written by Bob Dylan thirty years ago, are still
as relevant today. Sedated by political correctness and
chronically addicted to consumer goods, we have become
incredibly passive as a nation. The trouble is, we are too
passive to realise we are being passive! We seem to be in a
permanent dream-like state, whilst seismic shifts take place,
politically, morally and economically. Some critics,
primarily on the Right, claim that political correctness is a
Marxist-inspired effort aimed at undermining Western
values. Peter Hitchens wrote in his book *The Abolition of
Britain*: 'What Americans describe with the casual phrase ...
political correctness is the most intolerant system of thought to
dominate the British Isles since the Reformation.'

According to Lind and Buchanan, political correctness first
appeared courtesy of the work of the Frankfurt School - a
school of neo-Marxist critical theory, social research, and
philosophy at the University of Frankfurt, Germany in 1930.
It aimed to undermine Western values by influencing
popular culture through *'Cultural Marxism'*. Buchanan says
in his book *The Death of the West*: *'Political Correctness is
Cultural Marxism, a regime to punish dissent and to stigmatise
social heresy as the Inquisition punished religious heresy. Its
trademark is intolerance.'* We have to be very careful in our
use of the term. Some use it as a label to criticise anything
they don't agree with. If it is politically correct not to make
fun of people with disabilities, then I am politically correct.
I have heard evangelical preachers lay into political
correctness with gusto because they know that they will

receive roars of approbation from their congregation. It is an easy button to press.

In Part Three, I want to examine a number of areas where England has been destabilized and suggest that the erosion of a shared Christian consensus is the single most important factor. Whether you subscribed to the Christian faith or not, it was the 'glue' which held our country together until the mid 1960s; when this consensus began to implode it had far more profound consequences than foreseen.

I am not suggesting a return to a Mary Whitehouse style enforcement of morality, *'swatting flies, whilst ignoring the carcass'*. God forbid. If we examine the life and ministry of Jesus, he hardly ever paid any attention to the manifestations of evil he saw all around him; instead, he got to the root of the problem - the human heart. It was this that he tried to change. He was the least judgmental individual that ever lived, always trying to win and woo, to love the unlovely.

Chapter 13

The Road to Nowhere

'When the Son of Man cometh, shall He find faith on the earth?'

Luke 18:8, The Bible

THE ROAD TO NOWHERE

The decline of faith and the rise of unbelief can be traced from the 18th century to the early 20th century. As the Victorian era drew to a close, Christian theologian Ernst Troeltsch proclaimed that the sun was setting on Christianity, and poet Matthew Arnold declared that in the future poetry would replace religion. The 19th century provided the context not only for theories of God's demise but also for the numerous challenges that political thinkers, scientists and artists posed to Christian belief. Yet while the battles between faith and doubt were raging, church attendance did not decline but remained constant. The acceptance by intellectuals of Charles Darwin's theory of evolution is the most obvious single factor in this decline; the accompanying pain and confusion these intellectuals brought upon themselves eroded the social and spiritual foundations of their lives.

In the chapter 'God's Funeral' in Part Two, we have already looked at many of the thinkers and writers who contributed to the decline of faith in the pre-Victorian England; a little later, we will look at the various 'isms' that took root in the 20th century as old absolutes crumbled. Please note I am talking here about the decline of *faith,* not religiosity or churchianity manifested as hierarchical systems of control and repression. As Bono of rock group U2 has often said: '*I despise religion. Religion where I come from (Ireland) has so often been used as a weapon to beat each other over the head.*' Karl Marx was largely right when he famously said *'Religion is the opiate of the masses'* if by that we mean a set of rules and restrictions imposed by a hierarchical, tyrannical Church on its adherents, which has nothing to do with the Gospel of Jesus. The selling of indulgences, the tyranny of the Spanish

Inquisition are all manifestations of central control and repression imposed in the name of Religion. I am not talking about this, but rather the decline of personal faith in God.

The famous debates between Thomas Huxley, Darwin's 'bulldog', and Bishop Wilberforce contributed to an atmosphere of optimism about mankind and the world; Edward Gibbon's *The History of the Decline and Fall of the Roman Empire*, with its contempt of Christianity's 'highest ideals', and David Hume's sceptical *Dialogues Concerning Natural Religion*, which challenges the very possibility of the existence of the supernatural, provide the groundwork for the demise of belief in the 19th century. Professor Prabhu Guptara, a consultant on trends, recently made the interesting observation that it was the very grandchildren of the reformers who, not being given an intellectual reason for belief, were the ones who embraced the enlightenment and nurtured atheism etc.

Intellectual challenges to faith included George Eliot's translations of Feuerbach's *The Essence of Christianity* and David Friedrich Strauss's *The Life of Jesus, Critically Examined*; Darwin's evolutionary formulations, calling into question the idea of a special creation; Marx and Engels' charge that bourgeois institutions used religion to enslave people and make them weak; William James' reading of various religious states in *The Varieties of Religious Experience* as psychological states of mind. Alexander Solzhenitsyn wrote in 1976 about the West *'losing its soul. Great Britain - the kernel of the Western world - has experienced this sapping of its strength and will to an even greater degree than any other country. For some twenty years Britain's voice has not been heard on our planet; its character has gone, its freshness faded.'* The great Russian asserted that our troubles go back to the Enlightenment and the 18th century abandonment of the Christian faith, which acted as a social glue.

When any major thought system disintegrates, it gives rise to a fracturing and splintering which manifests itself in fragmentation. In the early years of the 20th century, this erosion of faith gave rise to a plethora of 'isms': variations on a theme, but essentially philosophical thought systems now made possible because Man is at the centre of the universe, God having been dethroned. I have said before that the 'worms' attacking The Sick Rose are essentially in the realm of ideas and so we need a working knowledge of these thought systems to understand better the journey we have been on as a nation. Not all of them are bad: there are many aspects of liberalism, for example, which make us a fairer and more tolerant society.

Humanism

By the middle of the 18th century, Jean Jacques Rousseau identified an agenda for humanism with his notable work, *The Social Contract*. Working with Voltaire, the humanists challenged the authority of government, church, and the new class of capitalist overlords with philosophies of justice and equality. Their writings spawned first the American Revolution and subsequently the French Revolution and similar revolts throughout the former Holy Roman Empire. The pulpit no longer held its dictatorial authority.

Early attempts to stem the tide of humanism, such as the Great Awakening from 1720 to 1750 with such powerful voices as Jonathan Edwards in America and the parallel activity of the Wesley brothers and George Whitefield in England only temporarily stemmed the tide. The impact of the great revivalists gave strong impetus to a worldwide missionary work with the slogan of *'Winning the world for Christ in our lifetime'*. The revival of Bible believers also gave rise to systematic scholarship, developing strong research tools such as concordances and verse-by-verse scriptural commentaries.

Liberalism

In the meantime other religionists, tired of denominational feuding and unable to accept the superstitious creeds of the Dark Ages, found an outlet in a new scheme of biblical interpretation. Using such devices as form and style criticism, these Higher Critics denied the literal accuracy of the Scriptures, professing the Bible to be a book of high moral principles and mythical allegories. A growing technological explosion bred a formal educational structure where students were taught to challenge the assumptions of the past and to question all previous premises. Charles Darwin's *Origin of the Species* introduced the theory of human evolution, raising fresh challenges to the biblical account of man's creation, fall, and final destiny.

Existentialism

This line of thought held that there is no *absolute* truth; what is true for one person may not be true for another. In existentialism, the individual's starting point is characterized by what has been called *'the existential attitude'*, or a sense of disorientation and confusion in the face of an apparently meaningless or absurd world. Many existentialists have also regarded traditional systematic or academic philosophy, in both style and content, as too abstract and remote from concrete human experience. Existentialism is a term that has been applied to the work of a group of 19th and 20th century philosophers who, despite doctrinal differences, shared the belief that philosophical thinking begins with the human subject – not merely the thinking subject, but the acting, feeling, living human individual.

Existentialism emerged as a movement in 20th century literature and philosophy, foreshadowed most notably by 19th century philosophers like Kierkegaard and Friedrich Nietzsche, though it had forerunners in earlier centuries. Fyodor Dostoevsky and Franz Kafka also described existential themes in their literary works. It gradually took form as a philosophical current in Continental philosophy during the first decades of the 20th century, becoming a widely known movement following the end of the Second World War, especially through the work of Jean-Paul Sartre and Albert Camus. Their work focused on such themes as *'dread, boredom, alienation, the absurd, freedom, commitment, and nothingness'* as fundamental to human existence.

Sartre's first novel, *Nausea* expressed the view that human life has no purpose. The protagonist, Antoine Roquentin, discovers that his own solitude induces several experiences of psychological nausea:

> *The rationality and solidity of this world, Roquentin thinks, is a veneer. Man can will nothing unless he has first understood that he must count no one but himself; that he is alone, abandoned on earth in the midst of his infinite responsibilities, without help, with no other aim than the one he sets himself, with no other destiny than the one he forges for himself on this earth.*

Albert Camus (from *Being and Nothingness*, 1943):

> *At the heart of all beauty lies something inhuman, and these*
> *hills, the softness of the sky, the outline of these trees at this*
> *very minute lose the illusory meaning with which we had*
> *clothed them, henceforth more remote than a lost paradise...*
> *that denseness and that strangeness of the world is absurd.*

Nihilism

Nihilism - from the Latin *nihil*, nothing - is a philosophical position that argues that existence is without objective meaning, purpose, or intrinsic value. Nihilists generally assert that objective morality does not exist, so subsequently there is no objective moral value with which to logically prefer one action over another; they claim that existence has no intrinsic higher meaning or goal. They may also claim that there is no reasonable proof or argument for the existence of a higher ruler or creator, or posit that even if higher rulers or creators exist, humanity has no moral obligation to worship them.

The term nihilism is sometimes used synonymously with anomie to denote a general mood of despair at the pointlessness of existence. Movements such as futurism and deconstructionism, among others, have been identified by commentators as nihilistic at various times in various contexts. Nihilism is also a characteristic that has been ascribed to time periods: for example, many have called our post-modern era a nihilistic epoch, and some Christian theologians and figures of religious authority have asserted that post-modernity and many aspects of modernity represent the rejection of God, and therefore are nihilistic. In most contexts, Nietzsche defined the term as any philosophy that results in apathy toward life and a poisoning of the human soul - and opposed it vehemently.

Nietzsche's deep concern with nihilism was part of his intense reaction to Schopenhauer's doctrine of the denial of the will. Nietzsche describes it as *'the will to nothingness'* or, more specifically:

> *A nihilist is a man who judges of the world as it is that it ought **NOT** to be, and of the world as it ought to be that it does not exist. According to this view, our existence (action, suffering, willing, feeling) has no meaning: the pathos of "in vain" is the nihilists' pathos - at the same time, as pathos, an inconsistency on the part of the nihilists.*

Nihilism, then, was in a sense like suicide and mass murder all at once. The nihilist continues to believe that only 'higher' values and truths are worthy of being called such, but rejects the idea that they exist. Because of this rejection, all ideas described as true or valuable are rejected by the nihilist as impossible because they do not meet the previously established standards.

A large scotch please.

Pessimism

Arthur Schopenhauer saw the worst in life and as a result was dour and morose; he was described as *'a lonely, violent and unbefriended man, who shared his bachelor's existence with a poodle'*. To Schopenhauer life was a painful process, relief from which might be achieved through art or through denial. *'The good man will practise complete chastity, voluntary poverty, fasting, and self-torture.'* Presumably any little bits of happiness we might snatch would only make us more miserable, such real and full happiness was not possible, *'a Utopian Ideal which we must not entertain even in our dreams'*. He was such an extreme pessimist that he thought we live in the worst of all possible worlds, constantly on the brink of destruction, and that happiness is an illusion.

Old Arthur was full of fun. He believed that our will, or our desires, are continually demanding things from the world that cannot always be satisfied, and so we are continually frustrated; even when our desires are satisfied it will only be brief. This satisfaction will then lead to an increase in our desires and, ultimately, to boredom when our desires are finally exhausted. Life, then, is suffering - an idea well known to Buddhists - and the answer for Schopenhauer was not to seek happiness, but to try and get through life with the minimum of suffering. The key to making life bearable for Schopenhauer was simply this: have extremely low expectations.

Relativism

Moral relativism encompasses views and arguments that people in some cultures have held for a very long time, such as the ancient Jaina Anekantavada principle of Mahavira (c. 599–527 BC). Protagoras' assertion (c. 481–420 BC) that *'man is the measure of all things'* might provide an early philosophical precursor to modern relativism; the Greek historian Herodotus (c. 484-420 BC) observed that each society regards its own belief system and way of doing things as better than all others. Various ancient philosophers also questioned the idea of an objective standard of morality.

In the early modern era Benedict Spinoza (1632-1677) notably held that nothing is inherently good or evil, but it is important to point out that his moral relativism did not make it necessary for Spinoza to become greedy or short-sighted; in fact, he lived a very peaceful, scholarly, and humble life. The 18th century Enlightenment philosopher David Hume (1711-1776) serves in several important respects as the father of moral relativism. He distinguished between matters of fact and matters of value, and suggested that moral judgments consist of the latter, for they do not deal with verifiable facts, but only with our sentiments and passions. He famously denied that morality has any objective standard, and suggested that the universe remains indifferent to our preferences and our troubles.

Common statements that might be considered relativistic include

- *'That's true for you but not for me'*
- *'Beauty is in the eye of the beholder'*
- *'You can't judge other cultures by the standards of your own'*

Moral relativism holds to the notion that some elements or aspects of experience or culture are relative to, i.e. dependent on, other elements or aspects. It is a world view and to determine where one stands on this issue, one must first determine what one believes about the origin of life. If you believe in an evolution which teaches that life is accidental, without meaning or purpose, anything you do is OK, because it ultimately doesn't matter. If you believe we are created, however, moral relativism cannot work. Creation implies a Creator. All things created are subject to a set of laws, whether natural or divine.

C. S. Lewis points to the nature of most quarrels as a clue to what we truly believe. Inherent in those quarrels is a concept of fairness, as in *'how would you like it if someone did that to you?'* When we make that statement, we are appealing *'to some kind of standard of behaviour [we] expect the other person to know about'*. In his September 19, 1796 Farewell Address to the nation, George Washington stated:

Of all the dispositions and habits which lead to political prosperity, Religion and Morality are indispensable supports. In vain would that man claim the tribute of Patriotism, who should labour to subvert these great Pillars.

Scepticism

Scepticism is both a philosophical school of thought and a method that crosses disciplines and cultures. Many sceptics critically examine the meaning systems of their times, and this examination often results in a position of ambiguity or doubt. This scepticism can range from disbelief in contemporary philosophical solutions, to agnosticism, to rejecting the reality of the external world. Philosophical scepticism is an old movement with many variations, and contrasts with the view that at least one thing is certain, but if by being certain we mean absolute or unconditional certainty, then it is doubtful if it is rational to claim to be certain about anything. Indeed, for Hellenistic philosophers claiming that at least one thing is certain makes one a dogmatist!

Agnosticism

Agnosticism is the philosophical view that the truth value of certain claims - particularly metaphysical claims regarding theology, afterlife or the existence of deities, ghosts, or even ultimate reality - is unknown or, depending on the form of agnosticism, inherently impossible to prove or disprove. It is often proposed as a middle ground between theism and atheism. Demographic research services normally list agnostics in the same category as atheists and/or non-religious people, using 'agnostic' in the sense of 'noncommittal'. However, this can be misleading given the existence of agnostic theists, who identify themselves as both agnostics in the original sense and followers of a particular religion. Philosophers and thinkers who have written about agnosticism include Thomas Henry Huxley, Robert G. Ingersoll, and Bertrand Russell. Religious scholars who wrote about agnosticism are Peter Kreeft, Blaise Pascal and Joseph Ratzinger, later elected as Pope Benedict XVI.

Bertrand Russell was a well known British philosopher of the 20th century. He was arrested during World War I for anti-war activities, and filled out a form at the jail. The officer, noting that Russell had defined his religious affiliation as 'agnostic' commented: '*Ah yes; we all worship Him in our own way, don't we.*' This comment allegedly '*kept him smiling through his first few days of incarceration*'. The term has come to be equated in popular parlance with scepticism about religious questions in general and in particular with the rejection of traditional Christian beliefs under the impact of modern scientific thought.

Atheism

Not all atheists are hostile to religion, but many do think that religion is bad. Here are some of their reasons:

- Religion gets people to believe something untrue.
- Religion makes people base the way they run their lives on a falsehood.
- Religion stops people thinking in a rational and objective way.
- Religion forces people to rely on outside authority, rather than becoming self-reliant.
- Religion imposes irrational rules of good and bad behaviour.

- Religion divides people, and is a cause of conflict and war. The hierarchical structure of most religions is anti-democratic, and thus offends basic human rights.
- Religion doesn't give equal treatment to women and gay people, and thus offends basic human rights.
- Religion obstructs scientific research.
- Religion wastes time and money.

Most atheists willingly concede there are some good things about religion, such as art and music, religious charities and good works. However, there currently seems to be an endless vogue for militant atheism, with angry, ageing men, scowling at us indignantly, competing with each other in demolishing the absurd notion of God. Christopher Hitchens glowers arrogantly at us via television appearances and through endless articles and book pages, militant in his certainty, unflinching in his regard for his own intellectual courage; in the grip of an ideology that is pretentious and muddled - pretentious in the sense of claiming to know more than it does. It claims to know what belief in God entails, and what religion, in all its infinite variety, essentially is.

Atheism is muddled because it cannot decide on what grounds it ultimately objects to religion. It claims religion is false and therefore it is harmful. But this is to make an assumption about the relationship between rationality and moral progress that does not stand up. Atheism is the belief that the demise of religion, and the rise of rationality, with man at the centre, will make the world a better place. As with Marxism, atheism has a fatal error at its heart - belief in the ultimate goodness of human beings. Marxian analysis was superb, until it was put into practice and produced grotesque dictators such Josef Stalin, Mao Tse Tung, Robert Mugabe, the list is endless. When one dispenses with God and His goodness, all you have left to believe in is Man, and his, er, goodness.

G. K. Chesterton famously said: *'If there were no God, there would be no atheists.'* Psalms 14:1 says: *'The fool hath said in his heart, there is no God.'*

Individualism

Individualism is the moral stance, political philosophy, ideology, or social outlook that stresses independence and self-reliance. Individualists promote the exercise of one's goals and desires, while opposing most external interference upon one's choices, whether by society, or any other group or institution. Individualism is opposed to collectivism, which stresses that communal, community, group, societal, or national goals should take priority over individual goals.

Whereas in the East, a person's primary identity is often to be found in his membership of family, tribe or social group, in the West the basic unit of society is the *Individual*, not the group. This has its roots in evangelical Christianity - at least from the 17th century onwards - with the emphasis on individual salvation and a man's personal response to the Gospel. Individualism is good if it helps us remember that each individual is unique and made in the image of God; individualism is bad when we are preoccupied with our own gratification - whether it be consumer goods, career advancement at all costs, sex, money or power.

Individualism is an over-riding feature of Western society and has produced untold misery: witness the breakdown of family, marriage and relationships, all fuelled by the notion that the individual has a divine right to happiness and must not let anything get in the way of fulfilling himself. It often renders parents impotent when dealing with their children: with the emphasis on children's rights, Mum or Dad is forced to back off from confronting behavioural issues which seventy years ago would have been swiftly sorted out by the creative use of a belt. Few would want to see a return to cruelty, but the pendulum has swung too far the other way.

New Age

Whereas these various 'isms' are not religious in that God is not at the centre, New Age is the nearest thing to a faith that we will find on the smorgasbord of post Christian philosophies, and as such deserves special mention in understanding where we have arrived as a nation. Unlike most formal religions, it has no holy text, central organization, membership, formal clergy, geographic centre, dogma, creed, etc. It often uses mutually exclusive definitions for some of its terms. The New Age is in fact a free-flowing, man-driven spiritual movement; a network of believers and practitioners who share similar beliefs and practices, which they add on to whichever formal religion they follow. Their book publishers take the place of a central organisation; seminars, conventions, shops, books and informal groups replace sermons and religious services.

The term *New Age* was used as early as 1809 by William Blake who described a belief in a spiritual and artistic '*New Age*' in his preface to *Milton: a Poem*; it was also mentioned by another Christian mystic, Emanuel Swedenborg, in the 18th century. Some of the New Age Movement's constituent elements appeared initially in 19th century metaphysical movements: Spiritualism, Theosophy, and

New Thought; also, alternative medicine movements such as chiropractic and naturopathy. These movements in turn have roots in Transcendentalism, Mesmerism and various earlier Western esoteric or occult traditions, such as the arts of astrology, magic, alchemy, and Kabbalah. The term *New Age* was used in this context in Madame Blavatsky's book *The Secret Doctrine*, published in 1888.

Neo-Theosophist Alice Bailey published the book *Discipleship in the New Age* (1944), which used the term *New Age* in reference to the transition from the Astrological Age of Pisces to Aquarius. Widespread use of the term *New Age* began in the mid seventies and probably influenced several thousand small metaphysical book and gift stores that increasingly defined themselves as 'New Age bookstores'. The term was further popularised by the American mass media to describe the alternative spiritual subculture – including practices such as meditation, channelling, crystal healing, astral projection, psychic experience, holistic health, simple living, and environmentalism; or belief in phenomena such as Earth mysteries, ancient astronauts, extra-terrestrial life, unidentified flying objects, crop circles, and reincarnation.

The New Age Movement includes elements of older spiritual and religious traditions ranging from atheism and monotheism through classical pantheism, naturalistic pantheism, to polytheism combined with science and Gaia philosophy. New Age practices and philosophies sometimes draw inspiration from major world religions: Buddhism, Chinese folk religion, Christianity, Hinduism, Judaism; with particularly strong influences from East Asian religions, Gnosticism, Neopaganism, New Thought, Spiritualism, Theosophy, Universalism, and Western Esotericism.

Go East

Meher Baba (1894-1969), who arrived in the U.S. in 1952 and opened a centre in South Carolina, was an author and teacher born to a Zoroastrian family in India. Mute from his twenties, perhaps as the result of being struck on the head years earlier, he communicated by smiles, gestures, and an alphabet board. He worked with the poor and insane in India in the forties, and his sometimes nebulous philosophy of 'spiritual value' and world harmony, resembling that of Yogananda, prefigured New Age. In the sixties, he strongly condemned the use of LSD and other drugs as a route to enlightenment.

The major Asian cult of the sixties was Transcendental Meditation, founded in India as the Spiritual Regeneration Movement by Maharishi Mahesh Yogi in 1957. The Maharishi brought TM to Hawaii in 1959, from which it spread to North America and Europe. His practice of deep relaxation, whose aim is 'bliss', was based on ancient Vedic literature that he claimed to have learned from his master, Shri Guru Deva. It was the Maharishi who was to influence the Beatles, especially George Harrison, who was a devotee of Hare Krishna until his death.

Age of Aquarius

Some astrologers claim that the dawning of the Age of Aquarius is correlated to various changes in the world and some claim that the early sixties were the actual beginning of the Age of Aquarius, though this claim is highly contentious. Common claims about the developments associated with the Age of Aquarius include, but are not limited to, human rights, democracy, innovative technology, electricity, computers, and aviation. There were several key moments in raising public awareness of this subculture: the publication of Linda Goodman's best selling astrology books *Sun Signs* (1968) and *Love Signs* (1978); *Hair: The American Tribal Love-Rock Musical* (1967) with the opening song *Aquarius* and its memorable line *'This is the dawning of the Age of Aquarius'*; the broadcast of Shirley MacLaine's television mini-series *Out on a Limb* (1987); as well as *A Course in Miracles* (1976) by Helen Schucman, *The Celestine Prophecy* (1993) by James Redfield, and *Conversations with God* (1995) by Neale Donald Walsch. Relevant works also include the writings of Eckhart Tolle, Barbara Marx Hubbard, Marianne Williamson, Paulo Coelho, Deepak Chopra, John Holland, Gary Zukav, and Wayne Dyer.

Paulo Coelho's *The Alchemist* has been read by millions and his books are sprinkled with Bible verses, mainly from the Old Testament. The book has gone on to sell more than 65 million copies, becoming one of the best-selling books in history: in total he has sold more than 100 million books in over 150 countries worldwide, and his works have been translated into 67 languages. He is the all-time bestselling Portuguese language author.

God for Coelho is almost a synonym for fate, or coincidence and he tells a good, if sometimes self-conscious, tale with plenty of folk wisdom thrown in for good measure. Since the publication of *The Alchemist*, Coelho has generally written one novel every two years. He has stated that he only starts writing a book after finding a white feather in the month of January of every odd year. This dates back to *The Pilgrimage*; while trying to overcome procrastination in launching his writing career, Coelho said *'If I see a white feather today, that is a sign that God is giving me that I have to write a new book.'*

159

Coelho found a white feather in the window of a shop, and began writing that day. Coelho believes that *'in the end all religions tend to point to the same light. In between the light and us, sometimes there are too many rules. The light is here and there are no rules to follow this light.'*

Chapter 14

Suicide of the West

'The timid civilized world has found nothing with which to oppose the onslaught of a sudden revival of barefaced barbarity, other than concessions and smiles.'

Aleksandr Solzhenitsyn

SUICIDE OF THE WEST

In 2009, Scotland released Abdel Baset al-Megrahi - the Libyan terrorist whose bomb blew up a plane over Lockerbie, Scotland in 1988, killing 270 people - in 2009. The ostensible reason for releasing him was compassion for a man terminally ill: a sign of a compassionate, enlightened democracy. It is ironic that this atrocity was committed in Scotland, for exactly two hundred and fifty years ago another Scotsman, Adam Smith, said, *'Mercy to the guilty is cruelty to the innocent.'* It might be suggested that the Scottish administration seemed more concerned with being nice to the mass murdering terrorist than with the innocent people blown up by him. In ways large and small, domestically and internationally, the West is surrendering - by instalments - to Islamic extremists.

In 1900, most citizens of the West felt tremendous pride and confidence in their civilization. There was a strong sense, common to Americans and British, to Europeans and Canadians, to Australians and New Zealanders, of belonging to a vigorous, expanding, progressive, and exciting civilization, the best ever. Today, that sense has gone. Why? Not because of economics, external events, or external enemies. Despite the horrors of the first half of the last century, by most objective standards Western civilization has, since 1900, made great material, military, medical, scientific, and even political progress. Western civilization saw off its two most deadly and horrific enemies, the Nazis and the communists, both of whom had been incubated in the West. If there is a crisis of the West, it is *internally* generated. It lies in the West's collapse in self-confidence. It lies in Western heads. It lies in *ideas*.

Western civilization has thrived more than any other civilization in the past or present - it has been much more successful in economic, military, and political terms, in science and technology, in the arts, and in enhancing its citizens' health, wealth, longevity, and even, probably, their happiness. For all its many manifest and serious faults, the West attaches more importance than other civilizations have done or do to the sanctity and dignity of human life.

In 1895 Lord Acton confidently asserted *'Opinions alter, manners change, creeds arise and fall, but the moral law is written on the tablets of eternity.'* In the last century, however, the decline of faith in the West has been accompanied by soaring levels of cynicism, depression, hopelessness and mental illness. Robert Browning (1812-89) prophetically observed: *'we have moved from an age of faith diversified by doubt to an age of doubt diversified by faith.'*

Richard Koch and Chris Smith believe that the West's success can be traced to six pillars of Western civilization, or 'ideas' or 'success factors' - Christianity, optimism, science, economic growth, liberalism, and individualism. Careful examination of the six ideas reveals well enough the character and peculiarities of Western civilization. It also enables us to see, despite all the successes, what is behind the widespread lack of confidence in the West.

Christianity

First century *Christianity* was a highly original, strange religion. It proclaimed a personal God who cared about everyone, regardless of status, nationality, or gender. It

164

required its adherents to take responsibility to improve their lives and help the underdog. It held that God could empower the lives of individuals, leading eventually to the odd view of Athanasius, the 4th century theologian, that *'God became man in order that we could become God.'*

Optimism

From the dawn of Western civilization to the early years of the 20th century, the history of the West was also driven by another idea - that of increasingly prevalent *optimism* about humanity and confidence in our ability continually to improve the world. Optimism led to activism - actions designed to increase our understanding and control of the natural world. Optimism has always been pre-eminently a Western trait. As psychologist Richard Nisbett says: *'To the Asian, the world is a complex place... subject more to collective than to personal control. To the Westerner, the world is a relatively simple place... highly subject to personal control. Very different worlds indeed.'*

Science

The third of our pillars is *science*. More than any of the other five success factors, the triumph of science explains the West's current enormous lead over other civilizations in technology, innovation, living standards, and military might. Scientific achievement since 1900 has been more far reaching in both intellectual and practical terms than at any other time, crowning six centuries of amazing discoveries about nature and the universe. The achievements and discoveries were, and continue to be, overwhelmingly Western.

Economic Growth

About two hundred years ago, rather suddenly in historical terms, economic growth in the West became unstoppable. The history of mankind up to that point had been one of modest or zero growth; population and living standards were flattened by nature, above all by hunger and disease. Between 1750 and 1820, England entered the machine age. Machines brought automatic growth, a novel phenomenon, and with the steam engine and industry, growth spread rapidly throughout the West. The arrival of self-extending growth is arguably the most important change in human history, making humanity a biological success, able to live long and safe lives, and multiply numbers and living standards enormously.

Liberalism

Liberal civilization, compared to other civilizations, attaches greater importance to the sanctity and dignity of human life, to the education of all its people, to equality of opportunity, to the freedom of the individual and the full development of his or her talents, to the elimination of prejudice against individuals and groups, to the promotion of science and the arts, to the invention of better, cheaper, and more convenient products, to the relief of suffering, and to the essential equality of all humankind. Liberal society is not institutionally corrupt, or cruel; it is not ruled by the police or the military; it is not (at least in theory) hierarchical or bureaucratic; it is not only fully democratic, but there is a spirit of freedom, fairness, and respect for all citizens.

Power in liberal societies is decentralized. There is freedom of the press and other media; freedom for business to operate freely, constrained only by requirements of honesty and humane standards; and tolerance of unconventional behaviour as long as it does not harm others. The government is subordinate to the rule of law. The state exists to serve citizens, to increase their health and wealth, and to protect them from arbitrary force and oppression of any kind. Liberal societies do not believe in military glory; war is a last resort, primarily for self-protection. In practice, liberal states almost never declare war on other liberal states.

Individualism

If there is one defining quality of the West, which its protagonists and antagonists agree is central to its character, it is *individualism*. The rise and rise of individualism is the motif running through Western history from Christianity, to the Renaissance, the Reformation, and the growth of the modern economy and modern society. Western individualism has no similar roots in any other civilization.

Pillars of Doubt

The six pillars of Western civilization have one clear common characteristic. They have all been the subject of increasing doubts, some for the past few centuries, some more recently. Belief in some form of Christianity was pretty much universal up to the 16th century; now a large proportion of the population, especially in Europe, are agnostics, atheists, or devotees of non-Christian religions. Optimism is no longer prevalent, because the roots of optimism - belief that creation and humankind are ultimately good, and that history is the story of human progress - have withered. Belief in science has been undermined in the last century by science making the world *harder* to understand, and by evidence that science has raped the planet and given us weapons of mass destruction.

Liberalism has fewer enthusiastic believers today, weakened by the sense that many members of society are 'victims' and therefore not responsible for their actions, and by the new heresy of 'liberal imperialism', which believes in imposing democracy by force. Finally, individualism is very unpopular with many in the West, particularly amongst intellectuals, for its alleged tendency to fragment and atomize society.

If there is no longer a clear consensus about the virtues of the West's distinctive values, there are only two possible results. Either we wallow in doubt and division, and eventually evolve into a very different - almost certainly less attractive - civilization. Or we recover our nerve and our beliefs and move on to a more sophisticated view of our heritage, which nonetheless preserves its essential positive attributes. For the truth is that doubts about the West's main ideas have been vastly overplayed. It is possible to restate the essential ideas in a way that intelligent people of goodwill can rally around.

The liberating spirit of early Christianity; its invention of the inner self; its stress on individualisation, rejection of authoritarianism, and love in personal relationships; its demands for compassion and equality for the downtrodden; and its promotion of self-discipline and self-improvement, is something that should appeal to all Westerners. Christianity burst the banks of the organised Church, even of all religion. A sense of responsibility derived from thinking for oneself, and emerging from one's own struggles in life, is likely to be deeper than one derived from obedience to authority, and, whatever one's beliefs, to be closer to the spirit of Jesus.

Optimism and pessimism are fancies, not facts. 'Realistic optimism' can best be seen as a duty. Only by believing that it is possible to improve ourselves and the world is it possible to do so. Science and reason are essential for the best forms of civilization; belief in science is no less and no more than commitment to truth, as best we can establish and understand it. There can be no open and healthy civilization without commitment to truth and debate, based on reason, experimentation, and the scientific method.

There is a problem with economic growth. In spawning machine-based economies, the West may have led the world to the brink of ecological suicide. But a society without growth is both unimaginable and undesirable. The answer lies in the replacement of industrial capitalism with what we call 'the personalized economy', a process that is very well advanced in the United States and United Kingdom. The personalized economy is based on individual imagination, and uses far fewer finite resources than industrial capitalism. The 'green nightmare' can be solved. 'All' it requires is a hugely greater sense of the urgency and importance of doing so.

The dangers of individualism may be exaggerated. In the shift from hierarchical society to personalized society, individualists can and do build personal reciprocity and local community. Individualists create far more than they destroy. Individualism has always been, and still is, ethically exacting and gregarious. The basic character of Europeans and Americans is unlimited personal striving and aspiration. Westerners invented personal responsibility, the concept of the self, personality, and the obligation of self-differentiation. They are world-improvers and self-improvers, driven by passion and relentless energy.

There is another side of the coin: when individualism becomes selfishness, it leads to family and relationship breakdown and we see the isolation of the individual from society. But individualism originated from ancient Greek and early Christian influences, and the codes of behaviour thus evolved were far more demanding of individuals than any previously devised. Individualism and the service of society are deeply entwined.

Crossroads

In the West, we have reached a crossroads. Down one road, the road currently bearing more traffic, lies doubt, cynicism, unmitigated selfishness, indifference, recentralization, and aggression. This road could take many forms, from anarchy to neo-fascism, environmental collapse to a new American empire. All such forms, however, would mark the end of Western civilization as the democratic and individualistic ideal Europeans and Americans have imagined, nurtured, and drawn closer to over hundreds of years. Western civilization will not be destroyed by our enemies; but it may be destroyed by ourselves.

Down the other road lies a recovery of nerve; confidence in ourselves and our culture; emotional unity within America and within Europe, and between Europe and America, and with other European settlements; a society and civilization comprising a billion responsible individuals, bound together not by authority or coercion or unquestioned traditional beliefs, but by self-discovered and self-validated attitudes of personal striving, optimism, reason, compassion, equality, individualism, and mutual identity. This road is well paved and brightly lit; travelling it is not that hard. But it requires a change of direction.

Militant Islam is a threat. But the real threat is that Western liberal society will ***implode -*** and that the vacuum thus created will leave the field open for totalitarian ideology. Whether this comes in the form of neo-fascism or in the religious clothes of militant Islam, nature abhors a vacuum and something *will* fill the void.

Chapter 15

The Church of England

'The Church of England is like a benevolent old gentleman with half moon specs and worn leather arm patches, cradling in his hands a laptop computer full of divine secrets about the future.'

The Author

THE CHURCH OF ENGLAND

Against a backdrop of indifference, the battle of ideas and the decline of faith, we need to turn our attention to the good old Church of England. Under attack from within and without, it can't make its mind up about important issues such as ordination of women and gay clergy. Indeed, most Archbishops of Canterbury end up as referees, rather than leaders of the worldwide Anglican Communion.

The Church of England has some 16,000 church buildings, in 13,000 parishes covering the whole of England, as well as 43 cathedrals. Between 12,000 and 13,000 churches are listed and about 45 per cent of all Grade I buildings in England are churches. A recent survey carried out for the Archbishops' Council and English Heritage found that 86 per cent of those surveyed had been inside a place of worship within the previous 12 months, for a wide variety of reasons. This included people of all faiths or none. The survey also explored people's perceptions of church buildings, and showed how they are seen as historic places and local landmarks as well as places of worship.

It is a uniquely English institution, with those typical qualities of tolerance and compromise usually in evidence. Evangelicals squabble with liberals whilst hard line African bishops look on. The familiar symbols of Anglicanism - old church building, dog collar, cassock, marriages and funerals - still sit comfortably with the majority of the population. The Charismatic churches' emphasis on spending money on people rather than buildings is not understood by many, who see the building as the church. *'Where is your Church?'* is a question often asked of the newer churches, to which the enquirer may get a mini sermon on the people being the living stones. The Church of England is still the state Church - just. Perhaps a look at its current head will afford some clues to its identity.

Rowan Douglas Williams was born in 1950, went to Swansea and Christ's College Cambridge, where he studied theology, and studied for his doctorate at Wadham College Oxford, taking his D Phil in 1975. In July 2002, with eleven years experience as a diocesan bishop and three as a leading primate in the Communion, Archbishop Williams was confirmed on 2 December 2002 as the 104th Bishop of the See of Canterbury. He is acknowledged internationally as an outstanding theological writer, scholar and teacher; he has also written throughout his career on moral, ethical and social topics and, since becoming archbishop, has turned his attention increasingly on contemporary cultural and interfaith issues.

As Archbishop of Canterbury his principal responsibilities are pastoral - leading the life and witness of the Church of England in general and his own diocese in particular by his teaching and oversight; promoting and guiding the communion of the worldwide Anglican Church. In 2008 Doctor Williams hit the headlines by stating that adoption of some aspects of shariah law was inevitable in the UK: whilst he may or may not be correct, the fact this comment came from the head of the worldwide Anglican Communion doesn't exactly strengthen his hand.

In this media-savvy age, the Archbishop comes across as a gifted, but distracted, academic - out of touch with the gritty realities of life. He has, though, been prepared to take on the government, much to his credit.

An English Church

Let us remind ourselves briefly of its history. The roots of the Church of England go back to the time of the Roman Empire when a Christian church came into existence in what was then the Roman province of Britain. What eventually became known as the Church of England (the *Ecclesia Anglicana*) was the result of a combination of three streams of Christianity, the Roman tradition of St Augustine and his successors, the remnants of the old Romano-British church and the Celtic tradition coming down from Scotland and associated with people like St Aidan and St Cuthbert.

These three streams came together as a result of increasing mutual contact and a number of local synods, of which the Synod of Whitby in 664 has traditionally been seen as the most important. The result was an English Church, led by the two Archbishops of Canterbury and York that was fully assimilated into the mainstream of the Christian church of the West. This meant that it was influenced by the wider development of the Western Christian tradition in matters such as theology, liturgy, church architecture, and the development of monasticism. It also meant that until the Reformation in the 16th century the Church of England acknowledged the authority of the Pope.

A Reformed Church

At the Reformation the Western church became divided between those who continued to accept Papal authority and the various Protestant churches that repudiated it. The Church of England was among the churches that broke with Rome; the catalyst for this decision was the refusal of the Pope to annul the marriage of Henry VIII and Catherine of

Aragon. The settlement of 1689 has remained the basis of the constitutional position of the Church of England ever since; it endowed the established Church with a range of particular legal privileges and responsibilities, but with increasing religious and civil rights being granted to other Christians, those of other faiths and those professing no faith at all. As well as being the established church in England, the Church of England has also become the mother church of the worldwide Anglican Communion, a group of separate churches that are in communion with the Archbishop of Canterbury and for whom he is the focus of unity.

The history of the Church of England from the 18th century onwards has been enriched by the coexistence within it of four broad traditions, the Evangelical, the Catholic, the Liberal and the Charismatic.

- *The Evangelical tradition* has emphasized the significance of the Protestant aspects of the Church of England's identity, stressing the importance of the authority of Scripture, preaching, justification by faith and personal conversion.
- *The Catholic tradition,* strengthened and reshaped from the 1830s by the Oxford movement, has emphasized the significance of the continuity between the Church of England and the Church of the Early and Medieval periods.
- *The Liberal tradition* has emphasized the importance of the use of reason in theological exploration. It has stressed the need to develop Christian belief and practice in order to respond creatively to wider advances in human knowledge and understanding and the importance of social and political action in forwarding God's kingdom.

- *The Charismatic movement* has, since the sixties, become an increasingly important influence. It has emphasized the importance of the Church being open to renewal through the work of the Holy Spirit. Its roots lie in Evangelicalism.

The Kindly Old Gent of Anglicanism

The Church of England is like a benevolent old gentleman with half moon specs and worn leather arm patches, cradling in his hands a laptop computer full of divine secrets about the future. Whenever we write something off, God seems to delight in breathing fresh life into dry bones. And they don't get much drier than some areas of the state church.

The contrast between the old and the new is striking. The kindly old gent, from his dress and demeanour seems to be an anachronism; he has stubs of pencils in his pocket, a fountain pen staining an inside pocket and everything about him harks back to the past. The laptop, though, is state of the art and contains an amazing rainbow of secrets and signposts to the future. Interestingly, it contains no mention of the liberal/conservative debate currently raging but is full of radical plans for using existing church buildings in new and dynamic ways- *'making of old stones, new paths';* it also contains the blueprints for a Church which challenges the State in an open and vigorous way and predicts a return to the Church's role as primary agent of social care, rather than the State. Radical indeed.

Evangelical Anglicans are a significant, vocal minority in the country, treated by the kindly old gent of Anglicanism as a colourful and wayward young nephew, to be indulged but told to belt up when becoming too outspoken, especially on issues affecting personal conduct like abortion and ordination of gay priests. One of his weaknesses is that, being English, he dislikes confrontation and unfortunately the old boy has a doctorate in fudging issues. I am not sure that God is as bothered as the Church by the deep schism between Evangelicals and Liberals on social issues, although the hysterical public squabbles which divide the Communion are probably a little trying.

The 77 million member global Anglican Communion is fractured by divisions over the ordination of women and gay clergy; it has been splintering since 2003, when the Episcopal Church (the Anglican body in the U.S.) consecrated the first openly gay bishop, Gene Robinson of New Hampshire. Rowan Williams has tried to hold the fragile communion together, but many fear a split is inevitable. One of the reasons for the recent spate of defections from the Anglican Church to Rome may be that the Pope deals in certainties; although many profoundly disagree with Catholic teaching, the Holy Father does lead, rather than referee.

Writing in The Daily Telegraph, the former Bishop of Rochester, Michael Nazir-Ali, claimed the 'social and sexual' revolution of the sixties had led to a steep decline in the influence of Christianity over society which church leaders had failed to resist. He said that in its place, Britain had become gripped by the doctrine of *'endless self-indulgence'* which had led to the destruction of family life, rising levels of drug abuse and drunkenness and mindless violence on the streets. He said the Church's influence began to wane during the 1960s, and quotes an academic who blames the loss of *'faith and piety among women for the steep decline in Christian worship'*. He says Marxist students encouraged a '*social and sexual revolution*' to which liberal theologians and church leaders '*all but capitulated*'.

The bishop added that Christian hospitality has been replaced by the '*newfangled and insecurely founded*' doctrine of multiculturalism, which has led to immigrants creating '*segregated communities and parallel lives*'. He said many values respected by society, such as the dignity of human life, equality and freedom, are based on Christian ones. But he warned that without their Christian backbone they cannot exist for ever, and that new belief systems may be based on different values.

'*Radical Islamism, for example, will emphasise the solidarity of the umma (worldwide community of the Muslim faithful) against the freedom of the individual. Instead of the Christian virtues of humility, service and sacrifice, there may be honour, piety and the importance of "saving face".*' In an implicit criticism of the Archbishop of Canterbury's claim that the adoption of some parts of Islamic law is unavoidable, Dr Nazir-Ali said: '*Recognising its jurisdiction in terms of public law is fraught with difficulties precisely because it arises from a different set of assumptions from the tradition of law here.*' He said that the Church of England must retain its importance in public life even if it does not remain privileged as the established church. '*It is necessary to understand where we have come from, to guide us to where we are going, and to bring us back when we wander too far from the path of national destiny.*'

I have devoted a disproportionate amount of space to what Nazir-Ali has said because - whether one agrees with what he says, or not - the former bishop is at least trying to lead, rather than please, placate and referee. The Church in this country, however, needs to go on a course for improving self-awareness, because it just does not realise how plain reactionary comments like Nazir-Ali's can appear. Without compromising its beliefs, it needs to actively seek common ground with those it differs from and find fresh language to make its points.

Anglican Church - The Future

Now we have some idea of how the Anglican Church arrived at where it is today, what of the future?

It is clear that the debate over homosexual clergy and, to a lesser extent, the ordination of women will not go away. Indeed, we are already seeing the first formal moves to establish a theologically conservative group within the Church of England with the UK launch of the Fellowship of Confessing Anglicans in July 2009. The FCA was launched in Westminster in opposition to liberal shifts in parts of the wider Anglican Communion away from the central authority of Scripture and the uniqueness of Christ.

The Bishop of Chichester, the Rt Rev John Hind, told the gathering: *'The source of our present crisis is to be found in attempts to minimise the uniqueness of Jesus. If a new reformation is in the offing or even already underway it will be important to return to Jesus, the high priest and pioneer of our faith, and place ourselves under the judgement of His teaching and word. What is at stake after all is not religious opinion but the saving truth of the Gospel.'* The Bishop of Lewes, the Rt Rev Wallace Benn, said the FCA wanted to stop the Church from being divided *'by moving back to the core of our faith, the historic Christian faith'. 'We are a movement for the renewal and reformation and renewed mission focus of our church. We love our Church ... we're not going anywhere,'* he said.

Liberal Anglicanism has always given importance to balancing the claims of Scripture, Tradition and Reason and hence to accepting the inevitability of diversity within a single church. Jonathan Clatworthy shows very clearly what is at stake in today's debate within the Anglican Communion. Liberals in the Church of England have been exposed to jibes that they offer a watered down version of Christianity and have trimmed their sails according to the prevailing winds of secularism. He is highly critical of Rowan Williams and Tom Wright, Bishop of Durham, stating

> ....(they) seek to turn Anglicanism into an intolerant and exclusive sect. Both Williams and Wright show themselves to be dogmatic authoritarians. Their appeal to consensus is really an appeal to an unreflective dogma which refuses to take any account of current beliefs. If there is a theology of the church which is distinctively Anglican, it is without doubt the tradition which ...holds a balance between scripture, reason and tradition. The church must be less obsessed with itself, more concerned with the society in which it is set; less determined to defend everything it has inherited, more open to discoveries from elsewhere; less threatened by new challenges, more excited by new possibilities...

The battle lines are now drawn in what will inevitably be the final showdown between liberals and conservatives in the Anglican Church. If the two sides can't agree, the cracks which began to show over the ordination of women may well become an unbridgeable chasm and the church will split completely. The original catalyst was the row over the consecration of Gene Robinson in the U.S., but Clatworthy argues that it goes deeper than that, to the very roots of Anglicanism itself.

Why is the Church of England so Important?

The Church will find its voice again, but it will be a voice that many do not expect. Mary Whitehouse made morality the centrepiece of her campaigns: Jesus never did. He always had a third, more perfect way which treated people as individuals and it will be a renewed emphasis on love, not judgment, that will characterise the Church's voice. The Anglicans have a natural parish because the parochial system is woven into the fabric of English life. The newer churches can struggle here, although often one finds they develop relational networks which take the place of geographical proximity.

It would be very easy to simply write off the Church of England as an anachronism, a home of fudge and compromise with little to say to the English public. There is some truth in this, but God has not finished with it yet. It didn't have an auspicious start: because of the refusal of the Pope to annul the marriage of Henry VIII and Catherine of Aragon, Henry established the Church of England and promptly installed himself as Head. It has bumbled along over the last fifty years, and latterly a succession of Archbishops has ended up refereeing between the liberal and conservative wings, with no real leadership. It gets on the public's nerves by regularly asking for money to prop up its ageing buildings, whilst it has hundreds of millions of pounds in its investment portfolio. If there was the equivalent of Ofsted inspections for religious organisations, the C of E would have been closed down years ago.

Dem Bones

I think we can compare the Church of England with the dry bones of Ezekiel 37, when the prophet is commanded to...

Prophesy to these bones and say to them, 'Dry bones, hear the word of the LORD!' ....I prophesied as I was commanded. And as I was prophesying, there was a noise, a rattling sound, and the bones came together, bone to bone. I looked, and tendons and flesh appeared on them and skin covered them, but there was no breath in them. Then he said to me, 'Prophesy to the breath; prophesy, son of man, and say to it, "This is what the Sovereign LORD says: Come from the four winds, O breath, and breathe into these slain, that they may live".' So I prophesied as he commanded me, and breath entered them; they came to life and stood up on their feet – a vast army.

We write off the Church of England at our peril. Attacked on all sides - both from within and without - the kindly old gent of Anglicanism is taking a terrible battering and probably just wants a quiet and comfortable retirement. Desperate for young men and women to put themselves forward as candidates for ordination, he looks with quiet, patient desperation into the future. It is apparent from studying God's dealings with the children of Israel that things often became totally desperate before God stepped in: here is a parallel with post Thatcher England. Could it be that our sleeping churches are like the bones - that they will be infused with new life and once again become beacons of hope for a confused and weary nation?

I like to think that God sees the Anglican Church as a treasured old coat, patched and threadbare, that He just can't bear to part with. A bit like mankind.

Chapter 16

The English Character

'An Englishman would rather die than not say thank you.'
The Author

THE ENGLISH CHARACTER

The idea that the English have a national character sounds plausible enough, until you start to try to pin it down. Are the English the romantic, imaginative people of Shakespeare and Keats, or the efficient imperialists who lorded it over India and Africa? The introverts whose motto is *'No sex please, we're British'*, or the swingers of Carnaby Street and Cool Britannia? The sneering redcoats of the American Revolution, or the plucky Londoners of the Blitz? Is the archetypal Englishman John Bull, or Colonel Blimp, or Monty Python? Whoever he is, it looks like he has a split personality: he is an adventurous homebody, coldly sentimental, genteelly vulgar. As Daniel Defoe wrote more than three hundred years ago, *'...from a mixture of all kinds began / That het'rogeneous thing, an Englishman.'*

Peter Mandler, a historian who teaches at Cambridge University, suggests that the first step towards understanding any idea is to recognise that it has a history. The whole point of national character is that it is timeless, something that endures beneath changes in manners. But as Mandler shows, not only have the English never agreed on what their character is; they have not always even thought they had one, or needed one. To David Hume the superiority of England lay precisely in the freedom that made it possible for men to develop their individual natures, instead of submitting to a collective one. *'Of any people in the universe,'* he wrote, the English *'have the least of a national character.'* This Enlightenment view was profoundly cosmopolitan and optimistic. What made the English so enviable was not an innate character, which other peoples could only envy, but a set of institutions, which they could emulate.

Mandler mentions that this emphasis on English civilization, rather than English character, never completely lost its power. It helps to explain why, in the nationalist 19th century, the English never fell hard for those racial and national myths that were so seductive on the Continent. They did not have to be proud of their ancestors' blood when they could be proud of their ancestors' accomplishments. Racial thinking found little sympathy in Victorian culture, and the influence of Christianity, with its emphasis on the individual soul, worked against racism. In the late 19th century, when the eugenic movement found eager adherents in America, England was blessedly free from the desire literally to engineer its national character.

For most of the Victorian age, it was liberals who were most interested in defining national character - a striking contrast to the present, when the notion is much more congenial to conservatives. To this day, our most positive myths of Englishness invoke the resilience and courage of 1940. But in a surprisingly short time, wartime solidarity gave way to the individualism of the 1960s and after. Fifty years ago, attempting to define Englishness, T. S. Eliot wrote about *'Derby day, Henley regatta, Cowes, the 12th of August, a cup final, the dog races, the pin table, the dart board, Wensleydale cheese, boiled cabbage cut in sections, beetroot in vinegar, 19th century gothic churches, the music of Elgar'*. George Orwell, writing about Englishness in *The Lion and the Unicorn,* claimed: *'It is somehow bound up with solid breakfasts and gloomy Sundays, smoky towns and winding roads, green fields and red pillar boxes.'*

Paradox

The English national character is dualistic: one aspect is conservative, the other extroverted. The pub is a fine example of the conservative aspect of English character. The pub, unlike the bar in the U.S., is a focal point for the 'locals'. One goes to the pub for the same reasons one used to go to church: for fellowship and spiritual enlightenment. There is nothing flashy or plastic about most pubs. Many look like one's living room, full of plush, soft chairs, couches, a fireplace, and bright lights. When the pubs close everyone goes home.

However, there is another side to the English Character - the extroverted and the innovative. It was not the U.S. but conservative England that produced the Beatles with their long hair and sounds that have influenced a decade of rock musicians and adolescents. Out of straight middle-class families came the androgynous Mick Jagger of the Rolling Stones and David Bowie, whose popularity challenged sexual stereotypes of Western culture.

Moderation

If there is one trait that absolutely singles out the English it is their shared dislike for anyone or anything that 'goes too far'. Going too far, as the English see it, includes displaying an excess of emotion, getting drunk, discussing money in public or cracking off-colour jokes and then laughing at them noisily. Beyond the pale altogether is the man or woman who regales one with his or her titles, qualifications or money. To the English the proper way to behave in almost all situations is to display a languid indifference to almost everything, though one may be seething underneath. Even in affairs of the heart, it is considered unseemly to show one's feelings except behind closed doors.

John Major was initially very popular because he was the embodiment of the cautious, likeable and personable Englishman which the public craved after years of confrontational, strident free-market Thatcherism. He liked cricket, had a nice wife and we even excused the fact that he tucked his shirt into his underpants because it made him so, well, human and ordinary. Continuing the male clothing theme, most Englishmen will settle for a blue or white shirt; the English don't want to stick out from the crowd and in matters of dress have a pathological need to conform. A pink, yellow, or green shirt renders a chap 'unsound' - that is for continentals who also wear - gasp - brown shoes for business. Major was the provincial bank manager, not flashy like Michael Heseltine nor too brainy like Sir Keith Joseph. In a word he was... moderate.

Understatement

Understatement is still a characteristic of the English, especially true of the older generation of middle England. There is a received wisdom that you never discuss religion or politics in polite society. I was recently playing (badly) in a Church Cricket Festival in Bristol and at lunchtime there was an evangelistic talk given by a minor counties cricketer; although the audience were largely under forty, one could observe a number of 'displacement' activities taking place while he spoke for fifteen minutes: closing one's eyes because of the sun meant that embarrassed eye contact did not have to be made; gazing intently at the Festival programme suggested one was interested in the competition but had, as a matter of urgency, to check some administrative details. Directness about one's personal life is not in our DNA: it is a private matter and should be kept as such.

In Andrew Marr's BBC Radio Four series *Unmasking the English,* he said that the English were the only nation on earth where *'understated'* and *'patriotic fervour'* went hand in hand. The series looks at fictional characters that appear to typify English characteristics. Agatha Christie's Miss Marple was presented as an exemplar of English upper class understatement, self-deprecation and muddling that tactically conceals a steely intellect and purpose determined to see through to the end whatever it has undertaken. Mike Brearley, ex-public school and former captain of the England cricket team, fits the same mould. There is something quintessentially English about Miss Marple, a character for whom there is a great deal of popular affection. This sort of scenario is indeed typical of a form of English fiction – a particular manifestation of English culture – and there are many modern English dramas that take up the baton from Agatha Christie's heroine, e.g. *Midsomer Murders*, *Morse* or *Rosemary & Thyme*.

It is unsurprising that Evangelicalism has prospered in the U.S., where some might say that understatement may be at a premium. I don't think the Americans understand our cynicism about tele-evangelists flashing telephone numbers on the screen for donations; equally, we don't understand what we consider to be their naivety in falling for it. Just as there is a gulf fixed between the two nations in terms of the Atlantic ocean, equally there is clear blue water between us in our attitudes.

Understatement is a form of speech in which a lesser expression is used rather than that which would be expected. It is a staple of humour in English-speaking cultures, especially in British humour. For example, in *Monty Python's The Meaning of Life*, a suburban dinner party is invaded by Death, who wears a long black cloak and carries a scythe. He is the Grim Reaper; the party is over; the guests must all go with him. *'Well,'* says one party guest, *'that's cast rather a gloom over the evening, hasn't it?'* In another scene, an Army officer has just lost his leg. When asked how he feels, he looks down at his bloody stump and responds, *'Stings a bit.'* Whilst visiting a chic London club one night, American film star Johnny Depp was dismayed to find that his drink had disappeared. The photographer who had taken it (by mistake) soon found his ears in Depp's hands and his head being forced toward the floor. The photographer's response? He drily informed Depp that this *'is not the customary way of greeting people in England'*.

The English use understatement because they find it difficult to be direct and forceful in their opinions. We beat around the bush and pussyfoot around confrontation and hope that we will be understood by hinting at something being amiss. That is why it has never been easy in England to talk about personal faith. P. G. Wodehouse - as quintessentially English a writer as you could ever find - created the delightful *Jeeves and Wooster* series of light novels, made into a successful and long running TV series featuring Hugh Laurie as the hapless Bertie Wooster and Stephen Fry as the all knowing manservant Jeeves. Jeeves is a master of understatement: when his master is about to don an especially colourful outfit, the manservant enquires *'whether Mr Wooster is considering wearing the garment in public'*.

It is also interesting to note that several prominent English Christians began as Evangelicals but ended up High Churchmen: youthful enthusiasm giving way to a more private faith. Whilst George W. Bush would be far more upfront about his brand of simplistic, muscular Christianity, Tony Blair kept his religious cards close to his chest and his Press Secretary Alistair Campbell famously said *'We don't do God'*. Blair converted to Catholicism, preferring its ceremonial and liturgical certainties, although he is on record as disagreeing with the Pope on social matters.

Why study the national character? Are there clues here to the decline of faith over the last two hundred years? For the Englishman, individual liberty and freedom of speech may explain why we have never had a French style revolution; the English will say *'I profoundly disagree with what you say but will give my life to defend your freedom to say it'*. The English soil has not generally been conducive to extremes of any kind, like our weather. We have never responded well to authoritarian regimes and although it has been predicted by some that we will become an Islamic state within fifty years, it is hard to visualise the English meekly accepting the diktats of mullahs and conforming to the rigidity of clerical state control.

Two Edged Sword of Tolerance

Our national strengths can also be weaknesses. Our famed tolerance may be one of the clues: these days, we tend to major on the minority and give too little consideration to the (often silent) majority. Tolerance taken to extremes results in an over-sensitivity to and indulgence of minority religious groups without the same deference shown to the 'host' faith, i.e. Christianity.

The Christian community in England feels singled out for negative treatment, and the reactionary Daily Mail fuels the fire with titbits of information about the schoolgirl sent home from school because she wears a crucifix, whilst her Muslim sister may get away unchallenged with her symbol of religious identity. We have become paranoid about offending other faiths, a contributory factor in our Christian national identity being eroded. The English need to debate the question of whether they actually wish to be a 'Christian nation' or not. Is Prince Charles to be the 'Defender of the Faith' or 'Defender of faith'? This is a profound issue and one which may require a referendum, because it is that important.

When you conflate moderation with tolerance, you have a major aspect of our national character which militates against a free flow of spirituality. One could say that the 'spiritual airwaves' are not open when compared with somewhere like India, where spirituality is found on every street corner. The English don't respond all that well to people who are passionate about their beliefs, distrusting outward displays of emotion. They will tend to switch off and may be more likely to read a pamphlet than listen to a speaker. It is not easy to share one's faith in England, and older Christians will, in the main, feel that it is a private affair. This national characteristic has unwittingly facilitated the dismantling of the Christian consensus over the last fifty years.

Another dilemma... whilst both the U.S. and England are characterised by individual liberty, why is Christianity so much more visible and popular in the U.S.? Again, I think the key lies in national character. The 'frontier' mentality of the early settlers in America meant that they were outspoken go-getters and this is part of their DNA. Evangelistic TV programmes popular in the U.S. would seem excruciatingly embarrassing to English audiences. In the U.S., therefore, whether one likes it or not, it is far more acceptable for faith and spirituality to be in the public domain. That said, American Christianity is often linked with the Republican right and, in more extreme form, fundamentalism, bombing of abortion clinics and angry posters informing us that fornicators will rot in hell. Because of our love of moderation, we instinctively recoil from extremism and perhaps that is why Billy Graham, the veteran American evangelist, has always been very popular over here: he is a gracious, thoughtful man of moderate views.

Parking Meters in Tehran

The pronouncement by Archbishop Williams that adoption of some aspects of shariah law is inevitable in the UK, seems, by implication, to suggest that the rise of Islam in this country is unstoppable and so we had better just prepare for it. I'm not suggesting that we re-enact The Crusades, but some causes are worth fighting - and dying - for and Williams appears too eager for accommodation with a religion and a culture which is alien to 95 per cent of the population. Again, it's that strange habit of not just accepting a minority but actively promoting it. Imposing shariah law on the UK, controlled by ayatollahs in Iran, would be like the London Mayor Boris Johnson having jurisdiction over parking meters in Tehran.

Please don't hear what I am not saying. Religious toleration is absolutely central to a civilized society and we should respect and tolerate other faiths. But actually *promote* them? People often ask whether Muslims and Christians can pray together: the cause of religious toleration would suggest that one should get the multi-faith handbills printed, but Christianity IS exclusive and the claims of Christ exclude other paths to salvation; logically then, if *'nobody comes to the Father but by me'* (Jesus' words) if we pray with those of other faiths, we pray to a different god.

The word 'exclusive' does not resonate comfortably with the English and some believers - me included - might prefer that Jesus had used more inclusive language - but He didn't. We confuse the term 'exclusive' with 'better' and Jesus wasn't making a value judgment: He was merely stating a fact. We need to reach out to other faiths - in as inclusive language as we can find - but not compromise our own beliefs in so doing. This is far from easy and we need the wisdom of Solomon. Muslims, Christians and Jews come together as people of the Book with Abraham, Isaac and others their common ancestors: but they come together *'neither as strangers or friends'*. This is at the heart of our difficulties.

I dislike intensely the 'Little Englander' approach to religious and racial matters but would argue passionately for a more balanced view which doesn't discriminate *against* the host culture and religion, that's all. There has to be a third 'voice' between the current alternatives: reactionary on the one hand, or passive and silent on the other hand. The trouble is, we haven't found it yet. We need to discover a fresh voice: one that states our perspective without ideological baggage, but with intellectual rigour, not emotion.

C. S. Lewis had this voice: as a world class apologist for the Christian faith, he marshalled his arguments clearly, without rancour or emotional baggage. We need theologians of Lewis' stature today who can make truth accessible to the man in the street, who understand the English national character and will write in a way that resonates with him. Already we are seeing contemporary theologians, such as Tom Wright (and American writers Rob Bell and Philip Yancey), putting across ancient truths in a highly accessible and inclusive style.

Death or Thank You

Evidence supporting my view that as a nation our tolerance and desire NOT to give offence is off the Richter scale can be found in everyday situations. An Englishman would rather die than not say thank you. We say thank you several times when talking to the shop assistant (often they don't warrant it), the taxi driver, the waiter; not content with this, we go into a decline if we don't say thank you several times to the kind motorist who lets us out in the queue, by a wave, a flash of the hazard warning lights, or a combination of both. Good manners are part of the English DNA but there is something frankly odd about our *preoccupation* with not giving offence. My Indian friends are bemused by this rigmarole, because it is generally absent in their culture; indeed, gratitude is implicit in Asian society and doesn't need to be expressed in words.

We love the underdog in this country - that's why we are such good losers - but our acceptance of diversity sometimes gets out of control and we end up with the aforementioned implicit promotion of Islam, for example. If we were an Islamic state then this would be understandable but - unless I've missed something - we're not.

We should feel proud of the fact that immigrants want to come here because we love diversity and freedom and they can join us in shouting at the Prime Minister, without our fingernails being removed or hands being cut off. Try that with Iran's cuddly Ayatollah Khamanei.......

How can we be robust without sounding reactionary? I haven't really mastered this yet. Attempts to suggest that immigrants of whatever colour or language should embrace the host culture are often labelled 'reactionary' and it seems virtually impossible to use some good old fashioned common sense without being branded a bigot. If we look back at what we have lost as a nation over the last fifty years, it is nothing short of disastrous.

Conservative Nation

England's innate conservatism is a major factor in the royal family having a far longer shelf life than other European nations. We write off the royals at our peril and my money would be on there still being a monarchy in one hundred years time. The revolutions which took place in mainland Europe in the 18th and 19th centuries were not mirrored in England: Christian historians point to the influence of John Wesley and the great evangelical awakening of the 1750s as the major reason that revolution did not take root in England. Whilst there may be some truth in this, an equally potent factor was the innate conservatism of the English character.

Socialism in the hands of the palpably sincere but wild looking, duffle-coated Michael Foot in the 1980s was never going to take root: it needed a smooth moderniser, Tony Blair, to make Labour electable in 1997 and what he served up was a reconstituted hotpot of conservatism, seasoned with a soupcon of politically correct sloganeering. Those on the Conservative left - the likes of Heath, Heseltine, Patten and others - could have slipped into the Labour front bench without any need for doctrinal change.

Europe

Should we be in or out of Europe? The question stirs up strong passions in most of us and is one topic guaranteed to elicit an opinion, and probably a forceful one at that. Why is there so much agonising and hand-wringing about this question which has preoccupied us as a nation for well over fifty years? Geographically we are in Europe - it is a fact. Culturally, most of us are not. The fact that we just can't decide perhaps owes more to our uncertainty over our identity as a nation than we care to admit, because if we were secure in our nationhood, becoming a fully paid up member of the European Union, currency and all, would be no big deal.

We have more in common culturally with our American cousins than our closer continental neighbours. To prove this you only have to land on the Normandy beaches as a booze cruiser to find out that the French just don't do things our way. We perceive them as haughty and unfriendly when they are actually very like us in character, even down to the understandable desire to speak their own language in their own backyard. Interestingly, although our allies in the two world wars of the 20th century where there was much mutual respect, we have always had an uneasy relationship with the French which may well go back to conflicts from the 19th century.

Eurosceptics would say that there are five factors in this ambivalence: history, geography, the economy, the social and cultural environment, and above all the British media. Anti-EU propaganda has, over many years, permeated deep into Britain's political culture and made a major contribution to the shift in British public opinion since the eighties.

The UK Independence Party (UKIP) demands full withdrawal from Europe and wants Britain's membership of the EU to be replaced by a host of trade and co-operation agreements; advocating a cross-Atlantic 'Free Trade Zone' with closer economic and/or political ties with the U.S. Nigel Farage, its former leader, said that the first permanent European Council president, Herman Van Rompuy had '*the charisma of a damp rag*', and compared the former Belgian Prime Minister to a '*low-grade bank clerk*'. Some of the reporting of Farage's insults was very indulgent of his rudeness towards foreigners. Little Englanders like UKIP relentlessly push the old patriotic buttons in place of rational argument - *'There'll always be an Ing-er-land', 'Britons never never never shall be slaves', 'Britannia waives the rules' (sorry, 'rules the waves'), 'This island race, this happy breed'*, Nelson, Trafalgar, Waterloo, etc.

Farage's outburst tells us much about how threatened some feel about Europe; one can just hear the conversation in the Home Counties saloon bar... *'he gave Johnny Foreigner what for did good old Nigel. That'll teach em!'*. It is fear that makes some feel the need to make unprovoked verbal attacks on our European neighbours; Van Rompuy had the wisdom and good grace to say very little in return.

Once we come to terms with the fact that we are no longer the major power we once were, hard-headed pragmatism would dictate that we align ourselves with one or other of two major power blocs. The trouble is, we are like the girl who can't make up her mind between two suitors: her head says Europe but her heart says the U.S. Embedded deep in the English psyche is our island mentality and somehow no amount of reasoned argument about the advantages of closer union with Europe seems to overcome it; the issue of a common European currency provokes strong reactions and we feel our sovereignty and independence threatened by such a move. Like Hamlet, we are as a nation full of self-doubt and our dithering over Europe suggests that we still have an identity crisis.

Daily Telegraph

The *Daily Telegraph* was the first penny paper to be published in London, founded in 1855 by Arthur B. Sleigh. In 1937 the *Daily Telegraph*, itself politically conservative, amalgamated with the *Morning Post*, the former conservative daily. Currently owned by the Barclay Brothers, it has a circulation of around 850,000, making it the largest selling 'quality' daily newspaper. The personal links between the paper's editors and the leadership of the Conservative Party, also known by the term Tories, along with the paper's influence over Conservative activists, has resulted in the paper commonly being referred to as the *Torygraph.*. However, in its early years it was associated with Gladstone and the Liberal party, coining the nickname *'the people's William'*.

We can learn much about the English character from studying the newspaper. Here we will find the values of moderation, understatement, tolerance and sympathy for the underdog; our traditional courtesy will manifest itself in a reluctance to criticise other faiths or cultures.

Sweet Charity

We are a kind nation. Especially kind to animals, the English have a developed social conscience which manifests itself in the existence of many thousands of charitable organisations, both large and small. It is interesting to note that many of the societies and institutions founded in the Victorian era live on today, but many have come adrift from their spiritual moorings. This may or may not be a good thing, depending on your point of view. Football clubs now in the English Premiership were originally founded as Church football teams (e.g. Southampton FC); the Young Men's Christian Association (YMCA) has reinvented itself as a primarily 'secular' institution with faith no longer a major factor. The Shaftesbury Society itself, although acknowledging its roots, operates as a 'secular' charity where personal faith is not a requirement for employees.

These changes are not all bad - quite the contrary. The essential ethos of the charity is usually preserved, but since a confession of personal faith is no longer a requirement, charities have a far wider potential recruitment 'catchment area'.

Cry of the Poor

Christians do not have a monopoly on compassion. Bob Geldof, Bill Gates and Anita Roddick are all 21st century icons, who, as far as I am aware, have no particular religious faith. They have heard the cry of the poor and responded to it. TV programmes like *The Secret Millionaire*, feature millionaires going back to their roots and seeking deserving individuals to whom to dispense cash; on a grander scale, Bill and Melissa Gates give billions to important projects, and *Live Aid* type events are part of the cultural backdrop. The young - and not so young - also want to give, but not always just via money donated to charities: increasingly giving their time and talents.

Some of the most passionate advocates of causes can be found in *Live Aid, Live 8* and various spin-offs: Bob Geldof's abiding passion for the poor of Africa was ignited whilst watching a documentary from Ethiopia in the mid 1980s. The Christian community needs to engage with mainstream, 'non-faith' charities, rather than separating themselves, which tends to happen. Some charities have become so large that the directors feel that methods more suited to double-glazing salesmen are now appropriate. Most Saturdays one can find fashionably dressed young people, often graduates, with clipboards in shopping malls the length and breadth of England, undertaking spurious 'surveys' which, surprise, surprise, end up with a question about supporting the charity by direct debit.

I have heard several stories of aggression when the request is politely declined, with a parting shot of *'so you're happy that those people will die then?'*. This is indefensible. I have also heard of reputable national charities telephoning individuals at random, stating *'our records show you made a donation to us seven years ago'*. In fact, you did nothing of the sort, but because it is so long ago you can't remember and it is a subtle - but dishonest - way of suggesting that perhaps you should do the same thing again!

Chapter 17

The Monarchy

'William and Harry needed (the Queen) more than hundreds and thousands of people keeping Kleenex in business.'

Dickie Arbiter, former Press Secretary to the Queen

THE MONARCHY

The death of Diana in 1997 was interesting. On one level, the floodwaters of grief which engulfed the nation were understandable: a beautiful, fragile princess which the nation had taken to their hearts, dying an undignified death in a Paris underpass, warranted great national grief. But was this all? I don't think so. Diana had become an international icon and her compassion had given her an almost religious aura: put simply, she was worshipped in the same way - and I am not being blasphemous - as the Virgin Mary. Pictures of Vishnu, Ganesh, Mother Theresa jostle for pride of place with a photo of Diana on many a Delhi taxi driver's windscreen.

The English have always been good at silence - at family meals spent wordlessly; intense emotions expressed through a hand on the shoulder - but on September 6th, 1997, they surpassed themselves. London, the big, braying capital, was stilled as over a million mourners of Diana, Princess of Wales, kept vigil along the route to Westminster Abbey. The hush amplified the sounds of the cortège as it set out from Kensington Palace: the rumble of wheels on tarmac, the clopping of horses' hooves, and a bell that tolled at listless intervals. But as the procession came into view, turning out of the palace gates onto the public road, a shriek pierced the morning air: *'Diana, my Diana!'* and then a despairing wail: *'We love you, Diana!'* Britain's customary stoicism had been overwhelmed by raw, unbridled grief.

Since Diana's death on August 31st, 1997, it is often said that the festival of mourning marked a transformation - the moment when the old British virtues of reserve and silent suffering, of *'mustn't grumble'* and *'could be worse'*, gave way to publicly expressed catharsis. The People's Princess had unlocked hearts, reordered values, presided at the triumph of emotional intelligence over cold intellect, of compassion over tradition. Thirteen years on, Diana is still the world's most famous Briton: she shook up the British monarchy and speeded its modernization. She helped to tear down prejudices about AIDS. She raised awareness of eating disorders. Diana remains an inescapable presence in British life: mostly, but not always, benign; a restless and seductive ghost.

Modernising the Monarchy

When the interviewer asked Charles whether he was in love, Diana's churlish fiancé replied *'whatever being in love means'*. Yet the Windsors thought they knew about love. It looked like patriotism. It was respectful and waved flags. It didn't sob on the streets or scream like a teenage girl glimpsing her rock idol. The quiet affection of the British people for Queen Elizabeth II has barely wavered during her fifty-four year reign. There was a low ebb early in 1998 - Diana's legacy - but even then the monarch's popularity rating dipped no lower than 66 per cent. It's now 85 per cent. Of course, there has always been dissent: some 18 per cent of Britons have called for the abolition of the monarchy since MORI, a polling firm, first began gathering opinions on the royals in 1969. That figure seemed as impervious to change as the Queen's fashion sense. Then Diana died and, for one week, republican numbers swelled.

In 2005 we witnessed Charles and Camilla's wedding, surely just the long overdue formalisation of a relationship which everyone knew had continued uninterrupted for thirty-five years. There was nothing glamorous about the event: the middle aged couple had many miles on the clock and Charles' thinning upper class haircut and expensive Savile Row suits couldn't disguise the essentially pragmatic nature of the day's celebrations. They possess a certain tweedy, upper class style, varnished with a seedy sheen which inherited wealth brings. The Queen muttered about Charles putting his personal gratification above princely duty - yet another example of royal doublethink where all that matters is not the substance, but the appearance of things. Interestingly, of late the relationship is reported to be increasingly fragile, Charles' petulance and selfishness becoming more pronounced the older he gets.

Why did Camilla come in for such a hammering? A cheerful, good-natured soul who is clearly indispensable to Charles, she was the subject of sustained vitriol in the popular press. She didn't break up the royal marriage - Charles did - and his response of *'whatever love is'* to the question *'are you in love, sir?'* on the occasion of his engagement to Diana has proved eerily poignant. Camilla has been seen by the English as the old boiler who took their magical princess away, the old tart in jodhpurs who took away our one remaining deity, Diana. The death of beauty and innocence seemed to coincide with political sleaze and turmoil, leaving a vacuum at the heart of the nation.

The Queen never gives interviews - a wise policy that has helped to preserve the fraying mystique of royalty. But as her subjects wept on the streets and dying flowers carpeted the sidewalks, Elizabeth's Trappist vow looked either boneheaded or stony-hearted. Dickie Arbiter, a former press secretary to the Queen says it was neither. *'The Queen was always going to pay tribute to Diana,'* he said, but she planned from the outset to make her broadcast shortly before the funeral. *'There was a furore because she was at Balmoral and not down with the snivelling mobs in London. [But] William and Harry needed her more than hundreds and thousands of people keeping Kleenex in business.'* The trouble was, the British people were not telepathic.

One hundred and fifty years ago, there was no issue over the monarchy: Victoria was adding *'Empress of India'* to her already substantial CV and the notion of getting rid of the monarchy was unthinkable. True, there have always been individuals and small groups who were virulently anti-monarchist, but in the past this has had little impact. Now it is commonplace to hear the subject debated in Rotary clubs the length and breadth of the land and a substantial (and growing) minority would be rid of the institution if push came to shove.

Uncertainty over our national identity is linked with this question. I don't believe for one moment that Charles, Camilla and the younger royals are any worse than their predecessors, as a cursory glance at the life of an earlier Prince of Wales, Edward VII (also known as *'Edward the Caresser'*), will indicate. It's just that their every move is recorded by intrusive paparazzi sticking telephoto lenses up the royal nostrils. Familiarity has bred contempt and many question the 'purpose' of the royals: it is no longer *'what is the monarchy'* so much as *'why is the monarchy?'*

A weak sense of national identity is the father of an insipid monarchy. Real power lies with parliament, but then it did back in Victoria's heyday so that can't be the root of the problem. There is a sense of foreboding... *'what happens when the Queen dies?'* is a very real, if largely unspoken, question. Republicans campaigning to topple the monarchy are buoyed by suggestions that Prince Charles wants to redefine the role of King. Claims by the Prince's biographer Jonathan Dimbleby that the heir to the throne wants to be free to speak out on major issues, if and when he assumes the throne, have given succour to those who think it is time for Britain to have an elected President as head of state.

Republic, a campaign group that counts prominent actors, MPs, writers, lawyers and others among its members, claims that Charles wants to take the country back four hundred years. *'The time is fast approaching when the future of the monarchy is going to become a major political issue,'* says the group's spokesman Graham Smith, *'It is clear Charles will not settle for the traditional role of King.'*

Defender of Faith

Prince Charles, when crowned king, has said that he wants to be styled Defender of Faith, whereas traditionalists would prefer that he stuck to the original job description compiled - albeit colourfully - by Henry VIII, which was Defender of **the** Faith. On the face of it, the loss of a definite article from a title carried by every English monarch since Henry VIII might seem harmless enough, but it is not. The edited formula will cause tremendous harm, not least because 'Defender of Faith' is too vague a phrase to interpret clearly. 'The Faith' in the original title is Christianity, originally Catholic, then Protestant; in recent decades it has been understood to mean Christianity in general. The Monarch's title is a specific recognition of his or her responsibility to preserve the unique, sacred status of Christianity in our society. To be sure, its importance is symbolic, but there are few more powerful things than national symbols.

In contrast, what does 'Faith' without a definite article mean? Sociologists are still unable, after two hundred years, to agree on a definition of religion. The same goes for faith. Prince Charles's intention is to extend his symbolic protection to members of minority religions - Judaism, Buddhism, Hinduism and Islam. Especially the latter, one suspects. How many times does the Prince have to be told that the pure form of Islam utterly rejects the notion of true religious diversity? And where, Your Royal Highness, do we draw the boundaries of the 'Faith' you defend? Is Scientology a proper faith? Is Spiritualism? Is the Church of Jesus Christ of Aryan Nations? How are you going to tiptoe through the theological and constitutional minefield created when unscrupulous, bizarre or extreme religions demand Royal protection - as they will? It is difficult to oppose Charles' line without sounding reactionary, but we do have to think very carefully as a nation before dismantling the specifically Christian heritage implicit in our Sovereign's title. It is tempting to hope that our present Queen will outlive her eldest son, fortified by her undiluted *Christian* faith and hereditary title.

Chapter 18

Materialism

'The triumph of shopping over politics.'
Andrew Marr

MATERIALISM

The national addiction to consumer goods is a major reason for our incredible passivity as a nation. The trouble is, we are too passive to realise we are being passive. With the erosion of a shared Christian consensus, the English now put their faith in materialism and are indifferent to major changes taking place. We seem to be in a permanent dreamlike state, whilst seismic shifts are taking place. The prevailing mindset of the English is that of materialism, in contrast to the Victorian age. This has had a major impact, not only on the English's hopes and aspirations but on their towns and cities. The heart is being ripped out of communities and is being relocated into out of town American style shopping malls. Without a religious consensus the pursuit of pleasure and leisure is what drives millions: just visit any shopping mall on a Saturday afternoon! Andrew Marr describes the current era as *'the triumph of shopping over politics'*.

One glance at the nation's TV programmes reveals a nation addicted to consumption and expenditure - and hence, debt. Because we live in dangerous times, in the shadow of terrorism and nuclear weapons, why not live now and pay later? If there is no heaven - as John Lennon famously and wistfully sang - then logically the pursuit of pleasure is all there is. Credit (or to be accurate, debt) is freely available, the more CCJs and poor credit history the better. Credit is your God given right - don't be without it. People that have shown themselves incapable of handling debt are being offered more - it's like the smoker dying of lung cancer being given even more cigarettes for Christmas. Crazy.

DFS, the furniture company, always on TV, offering free credit, nothing to pay for the first 12 months, further savings... they may as well give the stuff away. Debt counselling agencies are springing up all over the place: some offering a free service, others inviting you to take out more debt in order to clear existing debt.

Novelist J. G. Ballard in *Kingdom Come* describes the residents of an anonymous M25 commuter town as *'flocking to the Metro Centre shopping mall to worship at the temple of consumerism'*. Ballard says: *'We are a society without values. Politics is a racket. Patriotism is dead. The Church and the monarchy have lost what authority they once had. So what is left? All that we have left is consumerism. The real world is now this world of retail parks, where there is no sense of civic duty; where it's impossible to borrow a library book or to say a prayer. Where there are no art galleries, just consumerism.'*

Since as a nation our faith in almost everything has been eroded, our knee-jerk reaction is to put our trust in consumer goods, hoping that they will give us the warmth and comfort which we lack spiritually.

The Credit Crunch

In the summer of 2007 reckless 'sub-prime' mortgage lending to low-income Americans began a ripple of financial problems around the world. It made banks far less willing to lend to each other or to consumers. That's the crunch. This descended into a full-blown economic crisis in October 2008, following a rash of bank failures and nationalizations that swept around the world. Despite incredibly low interest rates, banks have still been reluctant to lend. The Government has pumped liquidity into the system through 'quantitative easing'; at the time of writing unemployment is still rising steadily and sovereign debt has been a major problem in Greece and Portugal; there is the possibility that the UK will lose its AAA credit rating. Unemployment has topped 20 per cent in Spain.

We are proud of the City. Proud of its reputation as the world's leading financial centre. Proud of the old city motto *'my word is my bond'*. But the bankers became greedy and have shown no real signs that they have learnt their lessons. As so many banks and building societies shed their mutual status and converted into public limited companies, their new owners - the shareholders - voraciously demanded ever greater, short term profits. To satisfy this, lending criteria were relaxed and it was not unusual for a married couple to borrow five times their joint annual income. Combine this with toxic mortgage debt in the United States and you have what veteran U.S. Investor Warren Buffett has termed *'financial weapons of mass destruction'*.

Perhaps William Blake's words are prophetic:

> *I see London, blind and age-bent, begging through the streets of Babylon, led by a child, his tears running down his beard.*

Babylon is a biblical symbol for money and materialism is the god of choice in the 21st century.

Wall Street Crash

There are similarities with the Wall Street Crash of 1929. Then, as now, a manufacturing boom based on rampant consumerism grew unchecked and eventually began to outstrip demand. The upshot was that along with stock market prices already pumped to exaggerated heights by punch-drunk investors, the value of shares was overestimated anyway. An adjustment, or 'correction', as it is now euphemistically called, was an inevitable necessity, but would it come too late? The issue of overinflation has been widely debated since, but it was certainly a growing concern for Federal Reserve members at the time. The body tried several times to stem the credit overflow by increasing discount rates and, in a move similar to the Financial Services Authority's ban on short selling in 2008, it outlawed what it saw as the practice undermining the market: the re-loaning of Reserve funds to brokers.

The rate cuts didn't work, and investors found other lenders willing to fund their ever increasing Wall Street forays. Resistance seemed futile; the Big Bull Market had become a national mania. Prosperity is more than an economic condition, though, it is a state of mind. It was here that things began to go wrong for the stock market and, unfortunately, a reaction did come too late. The lurches in late 1928 and the first half of 1929 should have served as warning signs for the more astute investors, but even leading economists of the day were betting that common stocks in the autumn of 1929 were a good buy. Everything was just going too well for it to fail. Even the great John Maynard Keynes bought shares in the months before the crash.

That opinion held until the market fell heavily on Black Thursday, 24th October 1929. Wall Street opened moderately steady in price but by mid-morning prices were falling through the floor. It was frightening enough that most of the gains made in the last six months had disappeared in a few short hours. The only answer seemed to be a desperate sell-off to rescue anything that was left. That day shares dropped by 13 per cent. Contemporary writer Frederick Allen summed up the swing of the markets beautifully: '*The gigantic edifice of prices was honeycombed with speculative credit... and was now breaking under its own weight. After a few flat days, the scales, which had been carefully balanced on the edge of collapse for months, had been tipped by some quick-fire share dumping and investors had panicked.*'

The response of the big banks will come as a familiar tale. Influential bankers from the top firms - J. P. Morgan and National City Bank amongst them – met for crisis bailout talks. They agreed to put up two hundred and forty million dollars between them as a pool to be invested in chosen stock and which, they hoped, would provide regenerative nourishment across Wall Street. Briefly, the bailout worked. Prices did hold over the weekend, but by Tuesday 29th of the following week much of those millions had been withdrawn and prices collapsed again. It was clear that investor confidence was drained and the market headed sharply downwards. The Stock Exchange was almost closed entirely, such was the chaos, but it was increasingly clear that it would take more than a mere stopgap measure to plug the now gaping holes.

Over the next two years prices sank an incredible 90 per cent and so began the Great Depression of the 1930s that would change the shape of the world forever. Unlike today, the government and financial authorities did little to resolve developing crisis, believing that the market would soon correct itself, and instead focused on maintaining a stringent budget. By January 1932 1,860 banks had failed in the U.S. - amongst them the huge Bank of the United States - and more would follow.

Chapter 19

Nostalgia

'We'll meet again... '
Vera Lynn

NOSTALGIA

To track the decline of the 'spirit' of England is like trying to catch the wind: but the broad sweep of history may come to our aid. As we have grown ever more prosperous materially, we have grown equally less prosperous spiritually. If God is dead, what is there left? Because in the West we have discarded the institution of the family like an old coat, all that seems left are ever more alternative lifestyles and individualistic materialism. There is a deep sadness in the heart of the English, an ache which is increasingly being assuaged by nostalgia, the explosion of interest in learning about our roots and tracing our family trees. I believe this comes from a desire to revive our spirits - and if this fails, we can always sublimate our feelings of loss by conspicuous consumption.

Peter Ackroyd identifies a tendency to look to our past as being peculiarly English. For us, romanticism, the past and the countryside are inextricably bound up together. It is tempting to think that these same ageless values inspire well heeled professionals to leave London for Gloucestershire, Devon and Norfolk. For some, no doubt, financial imperatives are important, but my hunch is that a subconscious desire for peace and tranquillity and more lasting, traditional values is the driving force. Although he may not be able to articulate it, Hugo is selling his 4 bedroom £950,000 house in Putney for a farmhouse in Gloucestershire because he wants to live in an England he perceives as closer to its roots. Implicit in his decision making is a gentle, wistful attempt to recreate the England of a vanished age.

An ageing academic observes in C. P. Snow's *The Masters* that '*nine out of ten English traditions date from the latter half of the 19th century*'. Among them are '*Sherlock Holmes, royal ceremonial, Gilbert & Sullivan and bacon and eggs*'. It is in the context of the late Victorian era that the foundation of the National Trust in 1895 needs to be set and understood. As David Cannadine writes:

> *Despite the pomp and circumstance of Queen Victoria's Golden and Diamond Jubilees, late nineteenth century Britain was in many ways an anxiety ridden nation and it was in response to such widespread feelings of uncertainty that these cultural and preservationist initiatives were launched.*

That is why the study of the Victorian era is so important in helping us understand the roots of England's decline. This anxiety led to a renewed interest in nature and history, which derived from the work of John Ruskin and William Morris. Cannadine again:

> *As the economic importance of the rural world diminished, its cultural significance significantly increased: witness Hardy's novels, Kipling's poems and Elgar's Enigma variations. These modes of expression differed, but their message was essentially the same: the rural past was preferable to the urban present, and the contemporary English countryside was idyllic yet beleaguered. It was idyllic because, in contrast to the squalor and deprivation of the towns, it was the very embodiment of decency, Englishness, national character and national identity.*

Pursuing this pastoral theme up to the present, TV series such as *The Last of the Summer Wine, All Creatures Great & Small, Dad's Army, The Darling Buds of May, Jam & Jerusalem* owe a lot of their popularity to the English countryside.

Bertie Wooster

Enter stage left P. G. Wodehouse's hero, the personification of Corinthian virtues: honesty, manliness, courtesy, chivalry, good humour - and not too bright. I believe there is something deeper in the nation's love of *Jeeves & Wooster* with its regular repeats on TV: once again, hankering after the solid virtues of an ordered and moral society, where boundaries were defined and people - especially servants - knew their place. Wooster is a bachelor with a private income, a minor aristocrat and member of the idle rich. He and his friends, who are mainly members of The Drones Club, are aided in all manner of societal adventures by the indispensable 'gentleman's personal gentleman', Jeeves. The gentlemens' clubs of London were a very important part of the genteel world of the twenties, and Wodehouse's satire of them is continuous and hilarious. While American club life tends to be business oriented, the British clubs are elegant clandestine establishments designed to serve as escapes form the responsibilities - and often the drabness - of their members' home lives.

Wooster's club is The Drones, whose exclusively upper class members are invariably shown in their beautifully furnished clubrooms jumping on sofas, playing catch with cricket balls, or throwing dinner rolls at one another. Jeeves' club is the Ganymede, whose equally exclusive membership is composed of butlers, valets, gentlemen's gentlemen, and others in the upper reaches of London's servant class. The Ganymede clubrooms are as elegant as The Drones', but the behaviour of the Ganymede members is impeccable. The club names themselves are a deft malicious touch. Drones, of course, are the stingless male bees that make no honey and live off the work of other bees. Ganymede, in classic mythology, is the cup-bearer to the gods.

Blackadder

The appeal of *Blackadder* is also interesting. The last episode of the last series, *Blackadder Goes Forth*, was superb pathos, with Edmund's boys going over the top, freeze-framed into oblivion; but it is the ordered world of the trenches and the nostalgia evoked that has made the series a real classic. Blackadder (Rowan Atkinson) is joined by the idealistic Edwardian twit Lieutenant George (Hugh Laurie), and their cook, Private S. Baldrick (Tony Robinson). General Melchett (Stephen Fry) rallies his troops from a French mansion thirty five miles from the front, where he is aided and abetted by his assistant, Captain Darling (Tim McInnerny), pencil-pusher supreme and Blackadder's nemesis, whose name is played on for maximum comedy. The comedy operates within a tightly proscribed social milieu where the class system thrived and a girl's honour was fiercely protected.

The final episode sees the main characters (Blackadder, Baldrick, George, and Darling) finally venturing forward and charging off to die in the fog and smoke of no man's land. Melchett remains at his office but blithely orders a reluctant Darling to fight with the others. *Goodbyeee...* had no closing titles, simply fading from the protagonists charging across no man's land under fire, to a field of poppies in the sunlight: like the poem *In Flanders Fields.*

Yes, M' Lord

Upstairs, Downstairs also merits particular attention. Set in fashionable Belgravia, Eaton Square, in the Edwardian era, the series ran for five lengthy seasons, totalling around eighty one hour episodes. The winner of countless awards, it has become a true classic of commercial television, and is still being seen in over forty countries by an estimated audience of three hundred million. Thirty years ago, when *Upstairs Downstairs* was first shown, the people responsible for creating the series were close enough to remember the reality of the world they were recreating, thus giving it authority and conviction. The production values now seem stilted and amateurish, but the series is excellent social history.

Hudson, the austere, clean living and pathologically snobbish Scottish Butler, is in many ways the pivotal figure. He mediates between the two worlds above and below stairs and acts as an agent of the established order, immediately quashing any attempts by the understairs staff to get too big for their boots, curtly suggesting that any attempt to rise from their lowly station is tantamount almost to treachery. Ruby, the dim and inarticulate lowest of the low scullery maid, is frequently the butt of Hudson's wrath, with the sound of the butler's reproach, (in a crisp 'Morningside' Scottish accent), *'get on with your work, my girl, and leave serious matters to your betters upstairs'*. Hudson has to tell his master that the cause of a disturbance below stairs is due to the *'valet trifling with the affections of one of the understairs staff'*. Not only does Richard Bellamy - the master of the house - depend on Hudson to ensure that the household runs like clockwork, but also that the social and class divisions are strictly enforced.

As the First World War gives way to the anxious and frenetic twenties, Hudson becomes dismayed as old class divisions are steadily dismantled. The cosy certainties of the old order are fragmenting, reflecting the erosion of social infrastructure in the wider society. Although this disintegration had a very positive effect on job opportunities for the working classes, it undermined the English sense of identity, rooted in the class system.

We'll Meet Again

The *Past Times* chain of high street shops sells nostalgia by the bucketload: music of the thirties, art deco jewellery, art nouveau china mugs, cookbooks from the fifties. The English desperately want to hang on to their past, trying to recapture the solid values and certainties evoked by items from the past. Alfred Dunhill, the Gentleman's tobacco company, has branched out recently into a whole range of upmarket thirties' products. The current management team undertook detailed market research and found that there was a growing market for high ticket items - across a range of products and themes - which played on the Englishness of the twenties and thirties. Gentlemen's motoring accessories alongside leather portfolios retailing at £250; gold pens, watches, clothing, all with the Dunhill branding. Nostalgia is big business. Jack Wills' chain of retro university menswear, Conway Stewart retro pens; the Rover 75, a Gentleman's Club on wheels with 1950s chrome and walnut dash board.

As well as being a land of churches, England is a land of pubs. Here again we see the same process at work: 'retro' themes everywhere, 'distressed' wood and millions of pounds spent on trying to make the surroundings resemble Biggles' local. For those who are too young to remember, Biggles was a very English fighter pilot, the fifties' creation of Captain W. E. Johns featured in many children's stories. I don't think it too fanciful to suggest that there is something profound at work here: the English are feverishly trying to recover and recapture the golden age when England's identity was solid and secure.

Brief Encounter

The simple story of an unrequited love affair between a suburban doctor and a middle class housewife, *Brief Encounter* is perhaps the most romantic film in the history of British cinema. It is an exceptional slice of English social history, with Celia Johnson and Trevor Howard agonising (well Celia Johnson anyway) over whether their clandestine love affair should be consummated. Noel Coward's magnificent screenplay conjures up the drab, emotionally repressed world of post World War II England better than almost any other literary text. Full of snatched conversations in dingy railway station refreshment rooms, in 1945 adultery was a serious issue and a daring subject for a film. Sixty-five years on, an audience would be bemused that a whole film could revolve around infidelity, a subject now thought of as insignificant, so far have social attitudes changed.

Ealing Comedies

The prodigious output of the Ealing Studios in West London during the thirties, forties and fifties is rich source material for the sociologist. Films like *Passport to Pimlico, The Lavender Hill Mob, Kind Hearts & Coronets* are quintessentially English, rather than British. Stanley Holloway, playing the archetype gentleman cockney with a backbone of good morals and manners; Dennis Price as the suave English aristocrat; George Cole as Flash Harry, the spiv... all recognisable stereotypes from another age.

There is an ache in the English heart. Vera Lynn, the 'forces' sweetheart' from sixty-five years ago still sings her heart out at annual VE day commemorations. For many, she is the symbol of a vanished England, one that many want to keep alive. Nostalgia is pervasive and powerful and I'm not sure that there is any other nation so spellbound by it.

The National Trust has over two million members and counting - easily the largest and most successful voluntary society in the Western world. What explains its extraordinary success? On one level, it is clearly a sensible way of ensuring that our national heritage is safe for future generations. But is it also an almost pathetic attempt to hold on to our former glories?

Chapter 20

The Thought Police

'Wriggly, malleable "ideas" which inhabit cyberspace: Peter
  Mandelson without a body, if you like.'

The Author

THE THOUGHT POLICE

The Thought Police are the secret police of Oceania in George Orwell's *Nineteen Eighty-Four*. It is the job of the Thought Police to uncover and punish *thoughtcrime* and *thought criminals*, using psychology and omnipresent surveillance from telescreens to find and eliminate members of society who were capable of the mere thought of challenging ruling authority. It also had much to do with Orwell's own *'power of facing unpleasant facts'*, as he called it, and his willingness to criticize prevailing ideas which brought him into conflict with others and their *'smelly little orthodoxies'*.

The term *'Thought Police'*, by extension, has come to refer to real or perceived enforcement of ideological correctness, or pre-emptive policing where a person is apprehended in anticipation of the possibility that they may commit a crime, in any modern or historical contexts. In the first half of the 20th century, the Special Higher Police in Japan were sometimes known as the *Thought Police*.

We are in the realm of wriggly, malleable 'ideas' which inhabit cyberspace: Peter Mandelson without a body, if you like. Political correctness grows from the soil of litigation culture and the ever increasing notion of 'rights'.

Ally Fogg in The Guardian:

> *Banning offensive words means people with vile opinions can hide their prejudice more easily. Let them speak and be judged. I think it reprehensible to use language that stigmatises, demonises and degrades whole sections of society. I agree that language informs attitudes and perceptions, and so influences behaviour, but that is not all. Language offers a window into the*

hearts of our fellow human beings. I, for one, am reluctant to see that window veiled.

People are perfectly entitled to use any words they like. I don't like the word 'chav' but I couldn't care less if someone uses it about specific deserving individuals, in a self-deprecating reference, or in a decent joke. She or he is also entitled to use it as a blanket catch-all shorthand for the poorest and most marginalised in society, or for the wider working class, and in return I am free to believe that such a person is a repugnant, heartless, supercilious snob. Similarly, anyone who uses a grossly sexist, racist, homophobic or bigoted epithet within my radar is unlikely to get a sympathetic hearing for the rest of our - probably short - engagement.

It simply does not help to have the likes of the Fabian Society or the Equality and Human Rights Commission laying down the latest list of forbidden words, with all the self-appointed arrogance of a Guide to Modern Etiquette. That totally misses the point. It is not words that sometimes need challenging, but the attitudes behind them. If we are not free to convey our honest beliefs, then our honest beliefs will never be challenged, and our conflicting opinions will never be fully explored. That cannot be healthy for any democracy, but worse - it actively undermines efforts to build a fairer, better society.

Rights Culture

The rights culture is second cousin to political correctness. In the sixties' deep South of America, Martin Luther King was battling for basic human dignity in suggesting that buses should be open to both blacks and whites, with no segregation. Because the white majority would not voluntarily make the correct moral choice, law and legislation eventually forced them to. This is the difficulty that lies at the root of any 'right' enshrined in law.

Most people would not argue with the notion of basic human rights. But there is a paradox at the heart of the issue. Once you start legislating against wrong-doing, you end up with a blunt instrument and some unexpected consequences. In 2005 a convicted paedophile successfully won £5500 in damages, arising from the stress which he claimed he suffered as a result of his prosecution taking an unreasonably long time. More recently, the Soham murderer, Ian Huntley, is suing the prison service for failing to protect him from a vicious attack in prison. There is a school of thought that would suggest that if one does wrong, one forfeits any rights. However, the relevant legislation was framed to ensure that the innocent didn't suffer: the trouble is, it also protects the guilty! The men in question clearly have little shame over their actions, otherwise they would have kept quiet.

The concept of rights tends to skew rational thinking so that black can become white and vice versa. Take brothels: in many countries, pragmatism has taken precedence over morality. The traditional Christian view of brothels would be that since their existence is based on sin - wrong practices disapproved of by the Creator - they must be closed down whilst reserving compassion and care for the individual prostitutes. Gladstone saw it as his mission to try to rescue 'fallen women' from their lives of degradation, with very limited success. The notion of licensing brothels, which is practised in some European countries, would have been anathema to him.

If we go along with the pragmatic view, we will uncover some anomalies. If there is no absolute morality, then earning a living as a prostitute is morally and qualitatively no different to earning it as a shop assistant. Shop assistants have rights, ergo so do prostitutes. Employment law would apply equally in the two jobs, so older prostitutes who lost their looks could logically sue their 'madam' if dismissed for this reason, on grounds of age discrimination. The taxpayer would foot the bill for legal aid. These days, because many would rather die than make a valued judgement, the notions of right and wrong, and hence 'sin', have fallen into disuse. The consequences have been incredibly profound.

Litigation Culture

At the same time as we became more 'permissive', the litigation culture of the U.S. was starting to drift across the pond. Litigation culture holds as one of its central tenets the belief that there is always someone to blame. The old adage *'that's just life'* cuts no ice with the aggressive, litigious lawyers of which the American Yellow Pages are crammed full. Trust between individuals has grown down, hence the phenomenon of prenuptial agreements.

Chapter 21

The Media we Deserve?

'I'm holding a bucket of s*** and tomorrow I'm going to empty it over your head.'

Kelvin MacKenzie, *The Sun*

THE MEDIA WE DESERVE?

It is difficult to discuss morality without sounding like Mary Whitehouse. A school teacher, alarmed at the tide of laissez-faire morality, Whitehouse founded the National Viewers & Listeners Association, again in the sixties. Frequently a figure of fun, she campaigned tirelessly - with mixed results. Branded a reactionary old killjoy, she attacked the symptoms of moral malaise tirelessly. Her cause was not assisted by her association with Labour MP Frank Pakenham, otherwise known as Lord Longford, who seriously needed to rethink his public image. When a society has become displaced from its roots there is no logical reason why it should be anything other than amoral and the homely moral watchdog might have had greater success if she had focused on the causes.

Tom Davies

In his first book *Merlyn the Magician & the Pacific Coast Highway*, Tom Davies describes a series of fearful visions he experienced whilst in Malaysia:

> *I had been working on a novel in the evenings. My themes were alienation, violence and arcane sexuality. The important point of the book, though, was not its plot but that, in the spirit of much 'contemporary' work, it was romantic. By a romantic I mean someone with a persistent attraction to the violent, the perverted, the morbid and the cruel.*
>
> *I was getting increasingly worried by the book. I sensed that, in some odd way, it was trying to tell me something. When I looked at my book again I saw a fungus ball growing*

out of it. It was one of the most amazing things I had ever seen. The ball glowed with a startling brilliant light with red, orange and purple veins running out of its heart and circling back into it. Ideas were trickling along the veins like tadpoles; faces moved around in it too. I understood immediately what the fungus represented. It was the poisoned and poisoning growth of my own romanticism; the dead and ugly vision which brings nothing but despair and decay.

Is Nothing Sacred?

I take issue with Christopher Hitchens' belief - entirely understandable, given his muscular atheism - that nothing is sacred, and further that nothing ought to be considered sacred. Thus, the only thing that should be upheld at all costs and without qualification is the right of free expression, because if that goes, then so do all other claims of right as well. Such a recognition need not lead to self-censorship or cowering dread of violence. Ideally, it helps a journalist depict people so accurately that they recognize themselves in the report.

I wish only that Hitchens' *style* of atheism did not drive him toward a campaign against sacredness as a category. Such a campaign only confirms the worst suspicions held by believers of various faiths, and it limits Hitchens' ability to understand the daily reality of billions of people. In the cause for free speech, Hitchens has more allies than he seems able to recognize.

In some ways, the media is too obvious a target for a book like this. One key question: does the media merely reflect changes in society or is it the instigator of those changes? One could agonise over this question for ages and the safest answer is probably a bit of both. Each generation asks the question *'is nothing sacred?'*: it is possible to detect within media output over the past forty years a steady erosion of ideas and subjects previously held sacrosanct. Media intrusion into the royal family's private lives led to the discovery of the highly embarrassing and excruciatingly intimate 'Camillagate' tapes, where the Prince of Wales expressed his desire to be so close to his beloved that he'd like to be a tampon.

A squirmy piece of royal trivia? Forty years ago, a newspaper editor would have thought it unthinkable to publish such a story, out of reverence and respect for the institution of royalty. Now it is fair game. In their remorseless drive to sell newspapers, do the editors of The Sun and the Mirror ever give a thought to their demolition of the sacred in our society? I doubt it.

There is general agreement that the press has become a pernicious and destructive force, aiding and abetting the erosion of standards. On the night of 'Black Wednesday', Kelvin MacKenzie, the editor of The Sun, telephoned John Major, Her Majesty's First Lord of the Treasury, the heir of Walpole, Peel, Gladstone and Churchill, and told 'John' breezily, *'I'm holding a bucket of s*** and tomorrow I'm going to empty it over your head.'* The next morning's front page read *'Now we've all been screwed by the Cabinet'*, an allusion lost on nobody whilst David Mellor retained his job. Clearly the editor of The Sun regarded himself as more important than the Prime Minister.

In 1969, The ailing Sun newspaper was bought by Rupert Murdoch, who soon turned it into a newspaper the like of which had not been seen before in England: screechingly vulgar, obscene and brutal. Australian Murdoch threatened everything Tory England should have stood for. He was ignorant of history, indifferent to English political tradition. As Karl Marx said: *'all that is solid melts into air, all that is holy is profaned.'*

Chapter 22

Militant Islam

'Muslim families have much to teach our nuclear, fragmented family unit about looking after each other, providing nurture and love within the extended family home.'

The Author

MILITANT ISLAM

Between the 7th and 12th centuries, Islamic civilization went through a successful military conquest period, but by the 13th century it went into decline and eventual disintegration as power and wealth slowly ebbed away under the inexorable advances of non-Muslim civilizations. The loss of this 'golden age' accentuated the sense of alienation and frustration and created deep-seated resentment and hatred towards Western civilization.

Militant Islam is a response from new generations of Muslims seeking to reclaim their supposed golden age, wanting to bring about the demise of Western civilization and the total imposition of Islamic rule over the world. Militant Islam distinguishes itself from any other contemporary political movement in the magnitude of its ambitions, seeking not just to influence the adherents of one religion or control one region; rather, it aspires to unlimited and universal power. Where have we heard that before?

Other elements of Militant Islam:

- Radical utopian vision akin to Marxism, Leninism and Fascism
- Totalitarian - seeing Islam as the absolute uncompromising control of all aspects of life
- Rejection of democracy
- Rejection of moderate views and aggressive elimination of those who uphold them
- Anti-Semitic
- Total destruction of Western civilization
- Absolute unwillingness to coexist

Conflict with the West

In the West, militant Islam seeks to exploit the hospitality, tolerance and security weaknesses of its host countries to spread its influence and objectives through the immigrant Muslim populations, with the goal of subversion of the Western powers and their eventual take over. They may appear law-abiding and reasonable, but they are part of a totalitarian movement and as such must be considered potential killers. Terrorism, in other words, is just one dimension of a war that has many fronts and takes many forms.

Violence is an important symptom of the problem, not the problem itself. Other methods might include acts of violence by loners, smuggling, rioting, lawful street demonstrations, raising money, teaching, proselytizing, intimidating, and even running for elected office. These methods complement each other, constituting the sophistication and reach of militant Islam. The battleground includes Muslim-majority countries as well as countries like Argentina where Islam is a minor presence.

The imams of Iran do not understand that Islamic law only applies within their own state. Dr. Michael Nazir Ali, who faced death threats when he said some parts of Britain had become 'no-go areas' for non-Muslims, said Marxism has been exposed as a nonsense but went on: *'We are now confronted by another equally serious ideology, that of radical Islamism, which also claims to be comprehensive in scope.'* Asking what weapons are available to fight this new 'ideological battle', the bishop said the values trumpeted by modern politicians such as *'respect, tolerance and good behaviour'* are *'hardly adequate for the task before us'*.

We must be extremely careful not to demonise all Muslims, the vast majority of whom are law abiding and peaceful, and who make a real contribution to our society. We need the wisdom of Solomon and the patience of Job in knowing how to deal with situations like the wearing in public of the burkha and niqab by some Muslim women. It is just too easy to reach for the emotional, knee jerk response.

Muslim families have much to teach our nuclear, fragmented family unit about looking after each other, providing nurture and love within the extended family home. It is no wonder that many Asians cannot understand our lack of respect for older people and our rapidly eroding morality.

Chapter 23

Fractured Society

'Eleanor Rigby, died in a church and was buried along with
her name; nobody came'

Lennon/McCartney

FRACTURED SOCIETY

It is apparent that there is not the same stigma attached to mental illness as there was in, say, Victorian times. High profile figures like Stephen Fry have done so much to get us talking openly about subjects which were previously 'no go' areas. The statistics quoted in this chapter indicate steady increases in anxiety and depression over the last fifteen years or so and one is tempted to come to the conclusion that mental illness is essentially a 'modern' disease. However, it is possible that levels of mental illness one hundred years ago were equally as high, for the simple reason that many families kept quiet about 'doolally' relatives and didn't have an emotional vocabulary to describe symptoms accurately.

It is also tempting to suggest that levels of fear have increased in proportion to the nuclear threat which started to surface in the fifties and sixties. Although it is impossible to measure levels of 'societal' anxiety, there is little doubt that we all live with a subliminal fear that the planet could be blown apart if the wrong person - and there are several suitable candidates, not least in Iran - gains access to the nuclear button.

Is it also fanciful to suggest that the erosion of the shared Christian consensus is a factor in greater mental illness? I don't think so. The collapse of any major thought system - whether Christian or otherwise - will surely lead to a fragmenting and fracturing of that society. Morality is often the glue that holds a community together, and when this is loosened both individual and corporate identity is weakened. It would be interesting to find out whether the incidence of mental illness is lower within faith-based communities.

Although I have no statistics to back this up, I have a sneaking feeling that levels of mental illness would have fallen during the Second World War, because of a very strong common identity and a shared moral consensus. In a sense, people didn't have time to be ill and maybe when one has more leisure, one also has more time for introspection. Depression is now very common and most people are directly or indirectly affected by it. We have looked at materialism in an earlier chapter and it is clear that increasing affluence has not made the English any happier.

Anxiety & Depression

A new report from the Mental Health Foundation reveals a UK society that is increasingly fearful and anxious, backing the latest national statistics that show a long term increase in the rate of anxiety disorders in the general population. An Office for National Statistics report shows that in England the rate of anxiety disorders in the population rose from 13.3 per cent to 15 per cent between 1993 and 2007. Applied to the whole UK population, this indicates that 7.2 million (1 in 7) people have anxiety disorders in the UK - 800,000 more than in the early nineties.

Mixed anxiety & depression is the most common mental disorder in Britain; depression affects one in five older people living in the community and two in five living in care homes. The report reveals that high levels of fear and anxiety are strongly linked to depression as well as a range of physical health problems including coronary heart disease, gastrointestinal troubles, asthma and allergies. Anxiety is also associated with unhealthy lifestyle choices such as smoking, drinking too much alcohol and poor diet.

UK-wide research carried out for the *In the Face of Fear* report shows that more than a third of people (37 per cent) feel more frightened than they used to and a majority think the world has become more frightening in the last ten years (77 per cent).

Family Breakdown

Children are increasingly suffering from mental ill health, a new report has found, with family breakdown a major cause. In the report, from the *Good Childhood Inquiry*, family relationships were identified as being central to children's well-being, with one author commenting that it's not just the event of family breakdown itself but the life that has to be lived afterwards that causes harm. The report was based on the responses of thousands of children to a recent study commissioned by The Children's Society. It found that one in four under-16s regularly feel depressed, with peer pressure and worries about physical appearance also listed as causes.

A poll of adults, conducted alongside the Inquiry, found that almost a third - 29 per cent - believed that family breakdown was to blame for harming children's well being. A fifth of those asked named peer pressure. One of the report's authors, Stephen Scott, Professor of Child Health and Behaviour at the Institute of Psychiatry, Kings College London, described how family breakdown can harm children's mental health. He said: '*It is as much about the problems arising from family breakdown as the event itself. Young people don't like being in different homes on different days of the week and get upset by strife between their parents.*'

The findings follow a recent spate of warnings from legal professionals, teachers and other experts that family breakdown is harming children. The Social Justice Commission also reported that children whose families break down often face a bleak future as a result. Mr Justice Coleridge, a High Court judge, recently said that family breakdown was among the most serious social problems facing British society, and tackling it should be placed at the top of the Government's agenda. He said: *'What is certain is that almost all of society's social ills can be traced directly to the collapse of the family life.'*

Fatherless Society

John Noble, in *The Shaking* asks:

Where have all the fathers gone? Fatherhood is a foundation of the Christian faith and is strongly linked to apostolic, prophetic and pastoral leadership in scripture. In the new Age of Aquarius, gurus tell us that humanity is coming of age. Emerging from the darkness and ignorance of 'Pisces', the era of the fish, we are to break free from the old patriarchal society to take control of our destiny. True, there are many chauvinistic elements of our culture that we would be well rid of. Male dominance, legalism, cruelty to women and children and the underprivileged, are wrong, but Luciferian New Age philosophy leads to rebellion and the collapse of society.

The last verse of the Old Testament - and a signpost towards the New - tells of Elijah coming to *'turn the hearts of the fathers to their children and the hearts of the children to their fathers'*. (Malachi 4 v 6).

Because of the individualism of the West, it is increasingly hard for fathers in the UK to discipline their children... *'If you smack me, you are infringing my human rights and I'll sue'*.

Instead, we are meant to be their friends; this emphasis on relationship rather than subservience is good, and I am glad that children no longer have to call their father 'sir' as in Victorian times - but the pendulum has swung too far the other way. Noble points out that *'the benefits of fatherhood are obvious as we look at the difference in behaviour between children in a secure family environment and those without'*. The sixties brought freedom - of a sort - but it fuelled rebellion and made the job of parenting, (difficult at the best of times), even harder.

Boomerang Children

One really interesting and positive development, largely brought about by economic factors, is that children are now living at home longer than before. *'The recent recession has been accompanied by a sharp increase in unemployment rates among young adults'*, states a report by Ann Berrington, Julie Stone and Jane Falkingham of Southampton University, published in a recent edition of *Population Trends*. The authors say that recent graduates, especially men, are increasingly returning to live with their parents after graduating. The meals are hot, the fridge is always full and the rent is low, so it is little surprise that more twenty - and thirty year olds - in England are living at home with their parents than at any time in the past twenty years.

The Office for National Statistics says many young adults in their mid-twenties and early thirties, and especially men, are increasingly postponing the transition to adulthood. In the past, British children have tended to leave home earlier than their European cousins but the latest ONS figures, at the time of writing, show that 25 per cent of men aged twenty five to twenty nine now live with their parents. This is almost double the proportion of women in their late twenties (13 per cent) who still live at home. One in three 'adult kids' who have not left the parental nest say they are still living at home because they cannot afford to get a toehold on the property ladder by buying or renting. But others, who have been dubbed kippers – kids in parents' pockets - are, say the demographers, staying through choice.

The demographers call this group the 'boomerang children'. Their numbers are being swelled by the increasing levels of student debt they have accumulated by the time they finish their studies; those with few educational qualifications are increasingly facing long periods of unemployment and can't afford to leave home. On the one hand, the massive expansion in higher education has seen the number of undergraduate students triple since 1970, from 414,000 to 1.27 million. On the other hand, the collapse of the youth labour market during the 1980s has been followed by a continuation of high unemployment rates despite periods of relative economic buoyancy.

The lack of jobs is being compounded by changes in the housing market. Even those in work cannot afford to move out of the family home as first-time buyers now face house prices that are, on average, five times average incomes, compared with a multiple of three times twenty years ago.

A Long Childhood

Children living longer at home are, in a sense, extending their childhood and David F. Bjorklund's *Why Youth Is Not Wasted on the Young: Immaturity in Human Development* extols the merits of a long childhood. He says that human development takes as long as it does for good reasons and that experiences should be introduced only when children are cognitively ready for them. He acknowledges that schooling is necessary for success in the modern world, but as much as possible, he believes, we should let children enjoy childhood. We should even seek to maintain some 'immature' qualities, such as curiosity and playfulness, into adulthood. As Aldous Huxley observed, *'The secret of genius is to carry the spirit of the child into old age, which means never losing your enthusiasm.'*

It may be too early to draw any major conclusions, but it is reasonable to expect that all this will have a beneficial effect on family cohesion in the UK. Perhaps we are starting to experience in the West what has been prevalent in Asia for centuries: because of economic necessity, Asian families have always been larger and stay together. As the economic pendulum swings towards the East, one can expect that the Asian family will gradually weaken with increased prosperity and mobility, whilst interestingly the Western family strengthens!

Technology

The rapid growth of the internet has brought many benefits, but also some unforeseen drawbacks. Because it is now easy to buy almost anything and everything via 'the net', the social interactions implicit in the old style market are vanishing and we are not aware of it. I know for myself that it is far easier to dash off an e-mail rather than pick up the phone. Multiply this by billions upon billions of internet rather than social interactions and you have one of the prime factors in social and relationship breakdown.

Since by and large the elderly have not bought into the computer revolution, they are becoming even more marginalised. True, there are 'silver surfers', usually middle class and affluent, but in the main the elderly have to purchase their goods and services from 'real' rather than 'virtual' shops. If this means the use of the local corner shop and social interaction, so much the better, but most of the shops are out of town now so again the elderly get a rough deal. Add to this the natural English diffidence and mistrust of strangers and you have a potent brew of alienation which renders pensioners lonely and impotent.

Chapter 24

Are the Prophets Silent?

'A prophet, almost by definition, doesn't fit into the categories you expect'

Eugene Peterson

ARE THE PROPHETS SILENT?

The Church is not very good at producing individuals who are equally at home both within the Church and wider society. The 'centre of gravity' of many Christians is wrong: it tends to be concentrated in the Church, rather than in wider society - which is biblical. Believers should be running mainstream bookshops, mainstream record shops, mainstream law firms, mainstream sports clubs and so on.

Christians often concentrate on building the Church, whereas Jesus said *'I will build my Church'*: the Church's job is to build the kingdom. There are lopsided churches throughout England which have been built by pastors, evangelists and teachers; whereas Ephesians 4 tells us that *'the Church is built on the foundation of the apostles and prophets'*. The pastor's heart is to look after the flock and this often militates against risk taking, which tends to leave apostles and prophets at a loose end, frustrated and unfulfilled. Prophetic ministry is, to be fair, often encouraged, but the prophetic voice is mainly confined within Church walls and has little opportunity to be heard in mainstream society.

Since it is clear from scripture that prophets are foundational, we desperately need the authentic prophetic voice to be heard in wider society; we have become cast adrift from our spiritual moorings and that incisive voice of compassion and hope needs to be heard. On the other hand, I struggle with books like Wale Babatunde's *Great Britain has Fallen!*, because I do not detect the spirit of Jesus. Instead we have the ramblings of a self-styled prophet addicted to exclamation marks! I was perturbed to see that so many Christian leaders had written positive testimonials.

'*The spirit of prophecy is the testimony of Jesus*', and so authentic prophecy should resonate with the voice of compassion and hope. Because true prophecy is so important, there are many counterfeits and often the prophetic ministry is discredited because it has been badly misused.

Christian Ghetto

This skewed centre of gravity produces the Christian 'ghetto' of Christian music, Christian dentists, Christian books. Nothing wrong as such, but it ignores the biblical imperative to '*go into all the world*'. Instead, a separate culture is created and one sees amusing juxtapositions such as the old lady who runs the local Christian bookshop trying to make sense of the Christian heavy metal band whose product she is required to stock on her shelves. It seems to me that God has been slowly dismantling this spiritual apartheid over the years and there is an increased understanding that believers should be found in all areas of life. Perhaps the recent unravelling of the Christian book trade is further evidence.

Back in another lifetime, I set up Ghettout Music (catchy name...) as a focus for young Christians into music to help them '*get out of the ghetto*' and ply their trade where everyone else did - in the mainstream. I am ashamed of many of the pompous, dogmatic pronouncements I made back in the early eighties, but I hope my heart was in the right place.

We will never produce authentic prophets from within the Christian community unless we allow them to grow in the real world, not some religious cul-de-sac. Prophets need a heart for the world, for the people, for society: this is why Bono had to grow up outside church circles, which tried to mould him and straitjacket him, when God had a much wider, more profound role and calling for him.

Around the release of their second album *October*, U2 were seriously considering disbanding. The leaders of the Shalom fellowship group they belonged to in Dublin had advised this course of action, believing rock music and Christianity were simply incompatible. A honest mistake - yes - but it highlights the need for Church leaders to be biblical in their thinking and to rely on God's word rather than cultural preference.

A few examples of prominent Christians who straddle both worlds are Jackie Pullinger, Patrick Dixon and Steve Chalke.

Chasing The Dragon

Jackie Pullinger graduated from the Royal College of Music having specialised in the oboe. She wanted to be a missionary, so she wrote to various missionary organizations. At first she wanted to go to Africa, but then she had a dream that impressed upon her the idea of going to Hong Kong. Unable to find support from missionary organizations, she sought advice from Richard Thompson, a minister in Shoreditch, who told her that she should buy a ticket for a boat going as far as she could get and to pray to know when to get off the boat. She followed his advice, went to Hong Kong by boat in 1966 and found work as a primary school teacher in the Kowloon Walled City; in the 1960s this was not policed and consequently had become one of the world's largest opium producing centres run by Chinese criminal Triad gangs. There, she established a youth club to help drug addicts and street sleepers.

Today, Pullinger organizes weekly meetings in the roughest Hong Kong neighbourhoods and offers shelter and rehabilitation to 200 heroin addicts, prostitutes, street kids and gang members. When her main centre is filled to capacity, Pullinger has been known to even rent out brothels to house the overflow. She offers shelter to what she calls 'uncared for' children, meaning their parents are absent because of work or drugs: she estimates Hong Kong has 130,000 such children. Prostitutes are given job skills.

But getting people off heroin is Pullinger's main objective. She doesn't use medication or phased withdrawal, but instead she places addicts in a room and gives them pyjamas. For the next ten days, they are prayed over and surrounded by a supportive group of recovered addicts who never leave them. In the end, she concedes that some addicts need at least five interventions before kicking the habit, while others fall somewhere in between.

Patrick Dixon

Patrick Dixon is a good example of a believer who successfully operates in mainstream society rather than just Church circles. He studied Medical Sciences at King's College, Cambridge and in 1987 was asked as a specialist in care of the dying to advise on the management of those with AIDS. He was deeply shocked by the poor treatment, prejudice and discrimination that many people with AIDS were experiencing from hospitals, clinics and community services. He launched the AIDS charity **ACET**, following publication of his first book *The Truth about AIDS*, which warned of an unfolding catastrophe that has since hit many nations in sub-Saharan Africa. ACET grew rapidly, providing home care services across London and other parts of the UK, as well as a national sex education programme in schools, reaching more than 450,000 students.

In the 1990s Dixon wrote several books covering a wide range of issues and trends including risk management, digital society, geopolitics, consumer shifts, health care, biotechnology, social issues, politics and business ethics. *Futurewise*, first published in 1998, uses the word FUTURE as a mnemonic standing for *'Six Faces of the Future'* which will impact every large business: **F**ast, **U**rban, **T**ribal, **U**niversal, **R**adical and **E**thical. He was named as one of today's fifty most influential business thinkers in a recent executive survey. Dr Dixon is an influencer, a prophetic voice in the areas of business, politics and social services.

Steve Chalke

Special Advisor on Community Action against Human Trafficking, Steve Chalke is a prominent, and often outspoken, Christian leader and social activist based in the UK, and an ordained Baptist minister. He is the author of numerous books and articles as well as a regular presenter and contributor on television and radio programmes. In 2004 he was awarded an MBE for his services to social inclusion by the Queen.

After graduating from Spurgeon's College in 1981 he set up Oasis Trust and it is now a significant voluntary sector provider, delivering services for local authorities and national governments, as well as self-funded initiatives aimed at providing opportunity to people across the globe. Steve has hosted his own television series' for ITV and BBC as well as presenting a regular show on BBC Radio 4. He is a regular commentator and contributor to television and radio programmes.

Chapter 25

Bono

'You broke the bonds
And you loosed the chains
Carried the cross of my shame
Oh my shame, you know I believe it'

Bono
I Still Haven't Found What I'm Looking For

BONO

I have devoted several pages to Bono of Irish rock band U2, arguably the most successful group on the planet. If you are not familiar with the band or their music - for reasons of taste, or age(!) - can I urge you to find out more about him, his song lyrics and charitable activities? Here is a current example of an individual making an incredible difference to the world, a real 'history maker'. The Church needs to discover and nurture more individuals like him, who have, to use evangelical parlance, a special 'anointing' and calling on their lives.

The Church expects true prophets to rise up from within its own walls, hence its great difficulty with someone like Bono - a Christian believer, with little or no church background but who knows his Bible very well. He was given the thumbs-up by the Billy Graham family, but why can't the Church see beyond the dark glasses, tobacco and f-words and see the heart of the man?

One of the hallmarks of the biblical prophet is his insistence on speaking truth in power, even when that truth is not particularly flattering or popular. Bono has used his platform as one of the most popular musical performers in the world to speak out against injustices in his native Ireland, in the United States, in Latin America, and perhaps most famously in his advocacy on behalf of the continent of Africa. A recent New York Times article noted that '*Bono's willingness to invest his fame, and to do so with a steady sense of purpose and a tolerance for detail… has made him the most politically effective figure in the recent history of popular culture.*'

Prophetic Voice

Eugene Peterson is a retired pastor of thirty-five years, Professor Emeritus at Regent College, author of over thirty books written primarily for pastors and, most famously, the author of a modern version of the Bible, *The Message*. To U2 fans, Peterson is known first and foremost as the guy whose Bible Bono likes. After the National Prayer Breakfast, Bono told reporters that he gets inspiration from reading *The Message* '*by the very gifted scholar and poet Eugene Peterson.*'

Peterson can hear, when Bono sings, the voice of the prophet in pop culture. When asked '*Is U2 a prophetic voice?*', he responded:

> *I rather think so. And many of my friends think so. If they do not explicitly proclaim the Kingdom, they certainly prepare the way for that proclamation in much the same way that John the Baptist prepared the way for Jesus... A prophet, almost by definition, doesn't fit into the categories you expect, which is what gives them bite, and clarity, and the sense of grabbing us by the scruff of our neck, and saying, 'Listen to this: this is truth, this is what's going on.'*

> *The whole authority of prophets comes not from what people say about them or the credentials that they have, it's from the truth of what they are saying. This is true of the Biblical prophets and of prophetic voices all through history. Often prophets use the name God but sometimes they don't. Bono's a good poet. He uses words in fresh ways and juxtaposes metaphors in ways that help you see things that you hadn't seen before. The songs all seem to be very expressive in collecting images and metaphors that are out of our lives. I guess the thing that makes them compelling is they don't use religious language. But you don't listen to them for very long before you realize we're*

working in the realm of God and relationships, of goodness and evil, and so suddenly he gets through our defences and we're listening to something that is very, very important to us but that we've insulated or inoculated ourselves against..

For example, in the song 'Peace on Earth': 'Jesus sing a song you wrote, the words are sticking in my throat.' Well, I start paying attention to that. And I love this line: 'But hope and history won't rhyme.' They are saying to me that I can't separate life into religious and secular, spiritual and ordinary: the dissonance between hope and history are the context in which we live life honestly and courageously, not by eliminating one or the other but by feeling or hearing that dissonance and living in a way that bring them into harmony. Bono's put two things together with 'Hope and history won't rhyme' which we usually keep apart, and they start working on each other, don't they? That's what poets do and what musicians do and that's why we need them.

And if they come from outer space like Bono and U2, then you take notice and appreciate it and thank God.

True prophets always stick close to scripture. Two excerpts from Bono's songwriting:

I believe in the Kingdom Come
Then all the colours will bleed into one
Bleed into one
But yes, I'm still running

You broke the bonds
And you loosed the chains
Carried the cross of my shame
Oh my shame, you know I believe it

Another song - '40' - taken directly from Psalm 40:

> *I waited patiently for the Lord*
> *He inclined and heard my cry*
> *He brought me out of the pit*
> *Out of the miry clay*
> *I will sing, sing a new song*
> *I will sing, sing a new song*
>
> *He set my feet upon a rock*
> *And made my footsteps firm*
> *Many will see*
> *Many will see and hear*

Humanitarian

Bono's first public involvement in humanitarian causes was through *Band Aid* and *Live Aid*, in 1984 and 1985. Fellow Irishman Bob Geldof spearheaded Band Aid after seeing horrific pictures of the famine in Ethiopia. He was so touched that he wrote a song featuring several pop stars, including Bono. This song went on to become the top selling single of all time in the UK, with proceeds all going to famine relief. Geldof's famine relief efforts continued through incorporating Bono and other stars in the Live Aid concert on July 13, 1985.

The U2 frontman began to get involved in various movements advocating humanitarian causes leading up to the new millennium. He joined Amnesty International and began to advocate for human rights injustices around the world. He also joined the Jubilee 2000 movement, fashioned after the Old Testament practice of cancelling debts in the year of Jubilee. This movement strived to get the World Bank, IMF, the U.S. and other wealthy nations to erase the outstanding national debts of 52 of the world's poorest countries in the year 2000.

In 2002 Bono founded the organization *DATA* (Debt, AIDS, Trade, Africa) to further advance his humanitarian pursuits. This organization continues to be active in lobbying developed countries around the world to relieve debts, fight the AIDS crisis, provide further development assistance and encourage fair trade. Interestingly, DATA also stands for Democracy, Accountability and Transparency. Overall, at the heart of DATA's mission is *'a view that these issues are not about charity, but about equality and justice'*.

Advocacy to Political Leaders

Bono's fame and work with advocacy groups has opened up avenues to interacting with the leaders of the free world. He believes that our political leaders have a responsibility to come to the aid of these countries. Instead of charity and a 'pay-off' to these countries, Bono aims to see these leaders comprehend Africa's plight, and give sacrificially, instead of token donations.

Bill Clinton

Through his efforts with the Jubilee Campaign, Bono made a case for third world debt relief. He lobbied for help specifically to former President Bill Clinton. In 2000, Bono appealed to the American government to encourage and increase debt relief to poor nations. His lobbying and persistence with Clinton paid off. Clinton became a powerful ally for his cause, asking *'Congress to provide $435 million to fund America's share of a proposal to drop the debt held* *by the world's forty poorest nations.'* Clinton commended *'Bono's passionate devotion'* as having brought together politicians of different persuasions.

George W. Bush

With the founding of DATA in 2002, Bono began his advocacy and friendship with George W. Bush. Much to the displeasure of his band mates he has allowed their relationship to become an article of public attention. When interacting with Bush, Bono appealed to the common ground of their faith, advocating biblical principles the United States should follow in assisting third world nations. Again, persistence has proved to be the key to success. Remarkably, since forming a relationship with President Bush, the United States has legislated aid packages for debt relief and the AIDS pandemic in Africa. In 2005 alone, President Bush designated over $1.4 billion towards relief, as well as an additional $674 million for Africa.

Tony Blair

Tony Blair, ex Prime Minister, earned praise from Bono for responding to appeals for African relief. Bono brought Blair's attention to the plight in Africa in an open letter addressed to him in 2004. In this letter Bono depicted a grave picture of a helpless continent desperate for aid from countries such as the United Kingdom. In it he says, *'Because 6,400 people are dying every day in Africa from AIDS...because over 100 million children in the world don't get to go to primary school...because every year 525,000 mothers die in childbirth - we urge you to increase dramatically the aid budget beyond the 2005 target of 0.4 per cent of national income and set a date for when Britain will meet its long-standing commitment to 0.7 per cent.'*

According to journalist Andrew Cave, this actually cemented the foreign aid agenda of the United Kingdom. Tony Blair has since made it an absolute priority to ensure poverty is the UK's first objective in foreign spending, resulting in a commitment to increase Britain's foreign aid budget by $25 billion per year. In conjunction, a deal has been brokered to eliminate debts of African nations.

Bono says:

> *They (the leaders of the world) should be afraid, because they will be held accountable for what happened on their watch. I'm representing the poorest and the most vulnerable people. On a spiritual level, I have that with me. I'm throwing a punch, and the fist belongs to people who can't be in the room, whose rage, whose anger, whose hurt I represent.*

Problems with the Church

It is no secret that Bono's spiritual journey has occurred largely in the absence of the Church. He is a lone warrior, disconnected from the larger body of believers. While petitioning Evangelicals for assistance on his Heart of America tour, he honestly informed them, '*I'm not so comfortable in the Church, it feels so pious and so unlike the Christ that I read about in the scriptures.*'

My own acquaintance with Bono began in 1981 when I was involved with the *Greenbelt Festival*, a major Christian Arts festival held over the August Bank Holiday weekend. I was promoting my record label, Ghettout Records, and there was something touchingly naive about his telephone call to the Greenbelt Office where he said '*The Lord has shown us to come- is that all right?*' It was all right and I was dispatched to pick them up with their guitars at the station and spent most of the day hosting them in my brother in law Dave Evans' tent. Since Dave and I were the only people at all familiar with their music, we found ourselves at the controls of the sound desk.

Bono had some harsh words back then for the Christian music press (especially *Buzz* magazine), who he said had betrayed a confidence, and his distrust of the Church and Christian circles can be traced back to those times. There is a need here for reconciliation. I spent a few days in Brighton after the Festival talking to Bono, The Edge and Larry about pastoral problems within the Band and was invited to several concerts. I also arranged a Musicians' Retreat in Worcestershire at which Bono and The Edge spoke and Bono said that the scripture that was foundational to the band, which described their calling, was from Isaiah: *'A voice of one calling - make a straight way for the Lord.'*

Despite the antagonism he has demonstrated for much of his career, in recent years Bono has appealed to the Church for its help, and found them to be surprisingly receptive. Looking inside the Church has undoubtedly softened Bono's heart.

> *I asked for meetings with as many church leaders as would have them with me. I used my background in the scriptures to speak to them about the so-called leprosy of our age and how I felt Christ would respond to it. Amazingly, they responded. I couldn't believe it. It almost ruined it for me - 'cause I love giving out about the church and Christianity. But they actually came through.*

Amos wrote poems, Jeremiah cried sermons, Isaiah alternately rebuked and comforted, and Ezekiel did street theatre. Bono writes songs and goes on tour, singing them.

Bono does not claim the status of a prophet, or announce a direct message from God; rather, he views himself as a sinful individual, searching for truth in a broken world. Billy Graham gives Bono his seal of approval and that's good enough for me.

Chapter 26

More Prophets

'It's a shadowy world, skies are slippery gray,
A woman just gave birth to a prince today
and dressed him in scarlet.'

Bob Dylan
Jokerman

MORE PROPHETS

Bob Geldof

Geldof? Surely a mistake? Not a believer as far as we are aware in the traditional sense, perhaps in the absence of any of God's people available for the task, God used the scruffy Irishman instead. That evening years ago, the Boomtown Rats singer watched the now celebrated documentary by BBC newsman Michael Buerk about the spread of massive famine in Ethiopia. The film, Geldof recalls, showed a relief worker selecting about 300 people from a crowd of nearly 10,000 emaciated figures. The 300 would be taken behind a wall and given a ration of butter oil to help keep them alive another few days. The others looked on in silence. A starving child simply leaned her head against the wall as flies buzzed around her eyes. *'I was utterly speechless that night'*, says Geldof, who since then has seldom been at a loss for a few hundred impassioned words.

Moved by a plague of biblical proportions, amid scenes of mass starvation, the scary Irishman threw everything he had at the problem - the showmanship of a space-age Barnum, the powerful simplicity of a messianic vision, the vocabulary of an outraged Teddy Boy, the passion of a punk prophet. Because of what he began the world reached out to untold millions. He clothed the naked and comforted the afflicted. He fed the children. He did the work of the Kingdom. He became, in short, 'Saint Bob', and at best that nickname offers an ambiguous homage, a tribute tinged with cynicism. After all, when he began his effort he was by his own admission just a run-of-the-mill rock singer and few imagined him capable of a startling metamorphosis into a very different animal indeed, into a lion of righteousness.

Bureaucracy Bypass

I remember some older Christians being more shocked by his use of expletives on TV than by the magnitude of the disaster. Within months Geldof had raised $11 million for emergency relief supplies. After an inspection trip to Ethiopia and Sudan, Geldof set up the Band Aid Trust and the global Live Aid rock spectacular in July, staged simultaneously in London and Philadelphia and broadcast around the world to an audience of 1.5 billion. It staggered the imagination in its conception and dazzled all in its execution, raising some $84 million and riveting more attention on the famine than all previous efforts combined. He became a master at bypassing bureaucracy.

Martin Luther King

Grandson of a slave, a fourth generation Baptist preacher, educated with a Ph.D., married and father of four children, Martin Luther King was a prophet who moved people with his vision and his words:

> *There comes a time when people get tired of being trampled by oppression. There comes a time when people get tired of being plunged into the abyss of exploitation and nagging injustice.*

Some years later in Birmingham, Alabama, when children were being jailed for non-violent civil disobedience, there were mass meetings night after night with King speaking, providing comfort to people, who worried about their children and themselves, their jobs and their lives. He spoke of their efforts as *'a tunnel of hope being dug through a mountain of despair.'* He preached constantly the message of freedom and human dignity.

284

Listen to the poetry in these words:

> *Look at what we've done.*
> *We've built gargantuan bridges to span the seas*
> *And gigantic buildings to kiss the skies*
> *Look at what we've done.*
> *But at the same time our people suffer...*
> *The iron feet of oppression*
> *Dark chambers of pessimism*
> *The tranquilizing drug of gradualism*
> *Dark and desolate valleys of despair while seeking sunlit*
> *paths of inner peace*

King was the Baptist pastor who said that his mission was *'to redeem the soul of America'*; he was a disciple of Gandhi, a student and an activist practitioner of non-violence. Nowhere is King's public theology of Christian unrest and resistance expressed with greater prophetic power and biblical authority than in the last sermon he preached from his pulpit at Ebenezer Baptist Church in Atlanta on 4th February 1968. It's entitled *The Drum Major Instinct* and explores the story of two of Jesus' disciples and their bid for greatness when they ask him for special honours in the Kingdom of Heaven.

King declared that the disciples shared with people the world over a definition of greatness based on what he called *'the drum major instinct'*. It's a fundamental human trait: *'a desire to be out front, a desire to lead the parade, a desire to be first'*. It runs throughout society, encompassing everyone from individuals and churches, to corporations and governments, affecting everything from racial and class prejudice to economic greed and international conflict. As far as King was concerned, the drum major instinct is the driving force behind the *'triple evils'* of racism, poverty and war. It is the root of sin, the heart of the human condition.

King is at his most prophetic and forthright in this sermon, warning America of the looming judgement of God - not just because of the war in Vietnam, but because of its arrogance and pride as a nation:

> *God didn't call America to do what she's doing in the world now. God didn't call America to engage in a senseless unjust war as the war in Vietnam. And we are criminals in that war. We've committed more war crimes than almost any nation in the world, and I'm going to continue to say it.*

Martin Luther King's words reached and touched every human heart who listened, even his adversaries. He preached concern for families, friends, and neighbours. He preached for those who worked for justice, freedom and peace. He preached for the victims of hunger, fear, oppression, and sorrow. Most of all, he preached for the freedom of his people. He spoke daily, often several times a day. We all know the *'I Have a Dream'* speech, his declaration made in the shadow of America's capital, but many have not heard the powerful, inspiring, moving rhetoric that he delivered day after day after day. He was a shrewd social strategist. He had the prophet's eye for seeing local injustices and the poet's ability to fit that local injustice into a transcendent truth. He believed, from the bottom of his heart, that things would change. He said over and over, *'We stand at the daybreak of freedom'*.

Jim Wallis follows in the tradition of King in stressing the values of love and justice, reconciliation, and community in his book *God's Politics: Why the Right Gets It Wrong and the Left Doesn't Get It*. He issues a clarion call to make both our religious communities and our government more accountable to key values of the prophetic religious tradition - pro-justice, pro-peace, pro-environment, pro-equality, pro-consistent ethic of life and pro-family - without making scapegoats of single mothers or gays and lesbians.

Bob Dylan

God don't make no promises that He don't keep.
You got some big dreams, baby, but in order to dream you gotta still be asleep.

When you gonna wake up, when you gonna wake up
When you gonna wake up, strengthen the things that remain?

Counterfeit philosophies have polluted all of your thoughts.
Karl Marx has got ya by the throat, Henry Kissinger's got you tied up in knots.

When you gonna wake up, when you gonna wake up
When you gonna wake up, strengthen the things that remain?

You got innocent men in jail, your insane asylums are filled,
You got unrighteous doctors dealing drugs that'll never cure your ills.

When you gonna wake up, when you gonna wake up
When you gonna wake up, strengthen the things that remain?

You got men who can't hold their peace and women who can't control their tongues,
The rich seduce the poor and the old are seduced by the young.

When you gonna wake up, when you gonna wake up
When you gonna wake up, strengthen the things that
remain?

Adulterers in churches and pornography in the schools,
You got gangsters in power and lawbreakers making rules.

When you gonna wake up, when you gonna wake up
When you gonna wake up, strengthen the things that
remain?

Spiritual advisors and gurus to guide your every move,
Instant inner peace and every step you take has got to be
approved.

When you gonna wake up, when you gonna wake up
When you gonna wake up, strengthen the things that
remain?

Do you ever wonder just what God requires?
You think He's just an errand boy to satisfy your
wandering desires.

When you gonna wake up, when you gonna wake up
When you gonna wake up, strengthen the things that
remain?

You can't take it with you and you know that it's too
worthless to be sold,
They tell you, 'Time is money' as if your life was worth its
weight in gold.

When you gonna wake up, when you gonna wake up
When you gonna wake up, strengthen the things that
remain?

There's a Man up on a cross and He's been crucified.
Do you have any idea why or for who He died?

When you gonna wake up, when you gonna wake up
When you gonna wake up, strengthen the things that
remain?

When you gonna wake up? is a stark warning to a sleepy, self-indulgent Church to stop compromising and instead *'strengthen the things that remain'* - once again to see the ancient words of scripture informing thought and action. Dylan has for millions been an astute and profound chronicler of our times and his songs captured the zeitgeist of the 1960s. Like Bono who came after him, Dylan has never fitted into the evangelical mould and thus, apart from his obviously 'Christian' phase, another towering figure has been largely overlooked by the Church.

From *Every Grain of Sand:* **'***In the Fury of the Battle you have to see the master's hand, in every leaf that trembles and in every grain of sand... I'm hanging in the belly of a perfect unfinished plan...'* This song suggests an artist often working within a strong Old Testament framework, who stresses the justice and obedience required by a sovereign God.

Blowing in the Wind captured the mood of the sixties perfectly: there was a new spirit of dissatisfaction with the status quo, exemplified by the anti Vietnam demonstrations in 1968. The Christian community took more notice of him during his 'born again Christian' phase, which resulted in the accomplished *Slow Train Coming* album - *'It may be the devil, it may be the Lord but you gonna have to serve somebody'* - and the poorer, propagandist *Saved* and *Shot of Love* LPs.

Dylan believed he had experienced a vision of Christ in his Tucson hotel room. *'Jesus did appear to me as King of Kings, and Lord of Lords. There was a presence in the room that couldn't have been anybody but Jesus... Jesus put his hand on me. It was a physical thing. I felt it. I felt it all over me. I felt my whole body tremble. The glory of the Lord knocked me down and picked me up.'*

Dylan's refusal to be pigeonholed has left him an enigmatic figure, but like all the very best artists, his songs contain truth: he holds up a mirror to Western society and reflects back much that needs changing. Dylan's discomfort with his role and his reluctance to speak, parallel the experiences of many of the Biblical prophets, who also felt uneasiness with their responsibility to warn Israel about the consequences of its unfaithfulness. Moses questioned God about his calling saying, *'O Lord, I have never been eloquent, neither in the past nor since you have spoken to your servant. I am slow of speech and tongue.'* Jonah famously ran in the opposite direction when God called him - ultimately landing himself in the belly of a whale.

In his autobiography, *Chronicles Volume One*, Dylan muses upon *'the big bugs in the press who kept promoting me as the mouthpiece, spokesman, or even conscience of a generation.'* *'That was funny,'* he says, *'All I'd ever done was sing songs that were dead straight and expressed powerful new realities.'*

Jokerman

I reproduce the lyrics of Jokerman below, since this is one of Dylan's more enigmatic songs, musing on evil, death, the Old Testament and a casual reference to the birth of the Messiah thrown in for good measure. It can be interpreted in several ways but is full of allegory and allusion.

Standing on the waters casting your bread
While the eyes of the idol with the iron head are glowing.
Distant ships sailing into the mist,
You were born with a snake in both of your fists while a
hurricane was blowing.
Freedom just around the corner for you
But with the truth so far off, what good will it do?

Jokerman dance to the nightingale tune,
Bird fly high by the light of the moon,
Oh, oh, oh, Jokerman.

So swiftly the sun sets in the sky,
You rise up and say goodbye to no one.
Fools rush in where angels fear to tread,
Both of their futures, so full of dread, you don't show one.
Shedding off one more layer of skin,
Keeping one step ahead of the persecutor within.

Jokerman dance to the nightingale tune,
Bird fly high by the light of the moon,
Oh, oh, oh, Jokerman.

You're a man of the mountains, you can walk on the
clouds,
Manipulator of crowds, you're a dream twister.
You're going to Sodom and Gomorrah
But what do you care? Ain't nobody there would want to
marry your sister.
Friend to the martyr, a friend to the woman of shame,
You look into the fiery furnace, see the rich man without
any name.

Jokerman dance to the nightingale tune,
Bird fly high by the light of the moon,
Oh, oh, oh, Jokerman.

Well, the Book of Leviticus and Deuteronomy,
The law of the jungle and the sea are your only teachers.
In the smoke of the twilight on a milk-white steed,
Michelangelo indeed could've carved out your features.
Resting in the fields, far from the turbulent space,
Half asleep near the stars with a small dog licking your
face.

Jokerman dance to the nightingale tune,
Bird fly high by the light of the moon,
Oh. oh. oh. Jokerman.

Well, the rifleman's stalking the sick and the lame,
Preacherman seeks the same, who'll get there first is
uncertain.
Nightsticks and water cannons, tear gas, padlocks,
Molotov cocktails and rocks behind every curtain,
False-hearted judges dying in the webs that they spin,
Only a matter of time 'til night comes steppin' in.

Jokerman dance to the nightingale tune,
Bird fly high by the light of the moon,
Oh, oh, oh, Jokerman.

It's a shadowy world, skies are slippery gray,
A woman just gave birth to a prince today and dressed
him in scarlet.
He'll put the priest in his pocket, put the blade to the heat,
Take the motherless children off the street
And place them at the feet of a harlot.
Oh, Jokerman, you know what he wants,
Oh, Jokerman, you don't show any response.

Jokerman dance to the nightingale tune,
Bird fly high by the light of the moon,
Oh, oh, oh, Jokerman.

William Blake

From penniless obscurity to recognition two hundred and fifty years after his birth as one of the greatest Britons, how did a mystical outsider like William Blake win a place in our hearts? William Blake was *'a bit of a nutter'*, to employ the vernacular of a recent prime minister. Or at least so some of his contemporaries suspected. While possibly falling short of diagnosable mental illness, there was always a degree of suspicion over a man who supposedly claimed to have seen an angel in a tree in Peckham Rye.

His poetry is taught in schools. Blake the marginal and Blake the crank have entered the art and literature establishment's pantheon. Blake the painter can be found on permanent display in Tate Britain. And it is not hard to read his name in a list that also features Constable, Turner and Gainsborough.

Jerusalem

The root of this popularity must lie at least in part in Blake's penning of the poem that became the hymn *Jerusalem* during World War I. Every couple of years somebody suggests making this song, with its *'chariot of fire'* and *'bow of burning gold'* into a national anthem for England. It is beloved of left-wingers, for the supposed social reform inherent in the *'dark Satanic mills'* reference, and right-wingers who see it as the ultimate piece of blazing patriotism.

Blake's masterpiece has been called both *'great'* and *'unfathomable'* by literary critics. Maybe, like Christ's parables, it takes a bit of work on our part to fully comprehend what is being said. The English don't like loose ends and yet Blake, like Jesus, left many of them and the poet, like Jesus, had little time for empty, organised religion. In his illustration *London* he imagines himself like the biblical prophet Ezekiel, walking round the streets of Jerusalem and seeing people disfigured with '*marks of weakness and marks of woe*', as a result of poverty, injustice, hypocritical social convention and the stranglehold of emerging capitalism.

Complex mythology

Beyond *Jerusalem*, there is a certain amount of love for William Blake as a classic English radical, someone who was the son of a hosier, came from the wrong class to be an artist and trained as a humble engraver. His image as being outside the mainstream has boosted his appeal. His work embraces a complex mythology involving struggling supernatural characters like *Urizen* and *Orc*, fantastic visions of rural England, allusions to English legends, criticism of slavery, and a healthy helping of Christian mysticism.

But William Blake, a paid up believer, was, from an orthodox standpoint, a rather unusual theologian, to say the least. At the end of *Jerusalem*, Christ is a unifying, all-encompassing entity: '*As One Man all the Universal Family; and that One Man/ We call Jesus the Christ; and he in us, and we in him/ Live in perfect harmony in Eden the land of life.*' The last work Blake embarked on as an engraver was his stupendous rendering of The Book of Job and one of his last notebook poems, worked and reworked, was *The Everlasting Gospel.*

George Richmond, writing to Samuel Palmer to tell him of Blake's death, reported that '*He said that he was going to that*

Country he had all his life wished to see & expressed himself
happy hoping for salvation through Jesus Christ.'

> To see a World in a Grain of Sand
> And a Heaven in a Wild Flower,
> Hold Infinity in the palm of your hand
> And Eternity in an Hour.

William Blake
Auguries of Innocence

Tom Davies

I mentioned Davies in an earlier chapter and he has never
been the same after writing his first book, *Merlyn the
Magician and the Pacific Coast Highway*, shortlisted for the
Thomas Cook Travel Book of the Year and later acclaimed
by Bono as being the *'one book that changed his life'*. He has
since written excellent books of pilgrimage but always
returns to the themes of violence, alienation and
immorality, culminating in *The Man of Lawlessness*. The
book attempts to examine what lies behind the upsurge of
lawlessness in modern society; Davies aims to show that
there is one mind and one philosophy generating the
current plague.

Examining the roots of modern alienation through the
Romantic writers, Davies traces how their philosophy has
influenced contemporary cinema and DVD, with its
consequent effect on behaviour, and draws parallels
between violent crimes committed on the screen and much
publicised real life atrocities. He exposes what he claims is
television's role in creating new acts of violence whilst
providing a psychological victory for the terrorist. He
looks at the way television has substituted true political

debate for hype; finally the author speculates that this threat to society was prophesied long ago by St Paul.

Davies, like Bono, does not fit comfortably into the evangelical idea of a prophet, but that is what he undoubtedly is. Very Welsh, fond of the sauce and a natural rebel, he is an accomplished and witty writer, flattened by the living God, a reluctant prophet who cannot 'unsee' what he has seen. He was close to David Watson, evangelist and Canon of York Minster before he died, which had a profound effect on him. Tom needs to be nurtured by the Church and I suspect his best work is yet to come.

Chapter 27

Where do we go from Here?

'Making of old stones, new paths'
Mike Starkey

WHERE DO WE GO FROM HERE?

In previous chapters we have examined the decline of the nation and my parallel assertion that this often converges with the decline of Christian faith. Although a process over the last two hundred and fifty years, five short years in the mid sixties accelerated this decline enormously and we are still reaping a bitter harvest from the well-intentioned, but flawed, social policies of the Roy Jenkins era. Ethical and moral foundations were being dismantled so fast that we are still catching our breath, fifty years on.

Not everything about the era was bad - far from it. I love the fact that we became far less stuffy as a nation and permission was granted for the English to start wobbling their top lip. A loosening of over-respect for authority was a good thing, but we have now gone too far the other way. As a nation we became more flexible, more fluid in our thinking; we allowed the East to challenge our buttoned up Teutonic thinking: it's a pity we didn't assimilate some of their superb ideas on the extended family as well. Mediterranean influences could be seen in outdoor café society and hugs began to replace handshakes, even amongst men.

It is not within the scope of this book to suggest too many answers; organised religion is often too quick to do this and I prefer to leave the reader with plenty to think about. It is my intention to follow *The Sick Rose* with a sequel, but in the meantime I have briefly sketched in a few topics which may repay further thought and discussion.

New Paths from Old Stones

What is needed is *re-engagement* with our past - rather than wallowing in nostalgia - as a compass for the future.

Ralph Waldo Emerson describes the English thus:

> *Courageous, large-natured, sensible; superficially morose, but at last tender-hearted; nothing savage, nothing mean resides in the English heart. No nation was ever so rich in able men; they are positive, methodical, cleanly, and formal, loving routine, and conventional ways; loving truth and religion, to be sure; they avoid pretension and go right to the heart of the thing. They hate nonsense, sentimentalism, and high flown expression.*

We need to rediscover those positive attributes that made us great as a nation and once again weave them into the fabric of English life. Patriotism without an enemy. Tolerance with firmness. Our Christian heritage once again being the backdrop to national life - without the double standards of Victorian morality.

God is always several steps ahead of us. We are all familiar with the Victorian chapel that has been turned into a wine bar: we sadly shake our heads, another reminder that our more robust spiritual past has been eroded. A tragedy, surely? Popping our head round the door we see it is a place of life and bustle, people enjoying themselves: it's a place that is being used, at the centre of town. Maybe it's God's way of showing us that the Church should be at the centre of the community, serving it, a place to be enjoyed, not endured.

God is in the business of recycling. Reusing old materials and making something even better. Old bricks are often used as hard core, foundations for a new and larger building. Old wooden church pews can be refashioned into dining tables. We are so earthbound that we miss God's aerial picture: things look very different from above the clouds.

I said earlier that the Kindly Old Gent of Anglicanism's state of the art laptop contains a treasure trove of secrets and signposts to the future: full of plans for using existing church buildings in new and dynamic ways; like a 3D chess game, it makes connections where previously none existed; it contains blueprints for the Church's major challenge to the State in areas such as poverty; it suggests new and undreamt ways of using the old stones of the parish system and making new paths. There are many new tricks up the old Gent's elbow-patched sleeve...

We saw in an earlier chapter how the Church in Victorian times was in the vanguard of social reform and care. Many of the great philanthropic movements which gave birth to so many social welfare agencies are still in existence today. We need to build on this, but in a way that is relevant to modern times. The Salvation Army still does great work, but is a bit of an anachronism: we need to see new organisations rise up, who are part of the digital age, but who have heard the cry of the poor.

Celtic Christianity

There has recently been a revival of interest in this subject. Our Celtic inheritance is a well worn spiritual path underpinning much of the Protestantism in this country which flourished during the five centuries leading up to the First World War. Celtic Christianity broadly encompasses the faith of Britain and Ireland before and during the sub-Roman period of the Early Middle Ages, when Roman withdrawal and the Anglo-Saxon invasion reduced contact with Continental Europe. It can be distinguished by its organisation around monasteries rather than dioceses and by traditions differing from those of the greater Christian world, most notably with respect to the monastic hair arrangement and the date of Easter.

There is little doubt that the life and times of the Celtic Church have been hopelessly romanticised in modern times, but by studying their beliefs, practices and priorities, the picture that emerges is of a vibrant, outward-looking church, with much to teach us today. Stories of miraculous happenings, perhaps embellished by overenthusiastic writers in later times, bear ample witness to this: healing, prophecy, hospitality and mercy seem to have been foremost among the spiritual gifts in operation. Much time was devoted to contemplative prayer and the development of personal holiness.

The Celtic Church encompassed a great care for all of creation: there was a particular concern for the poor, the sick and the oppressed. The Celtic Church had a great love for the scriptures, especially the writings of John and the Psalms. Much time was spent in copying, studying, memorising and teaching scripture. The Bible was their 'memory book', full of stories about God's dealings with his people and his mighty acts. Because Jesus was incarnate in the whole of life, no task, no situation was too small or unimportant for prayer. The hostile environment in which the church existed made the people aware of the reality of spiritual evil, and 'spiritual warfare' was part of their prayer life.

Here is a Celtic prayer:

> *Deep peace of the Running Wave to you.*
> *Deep peace of the Flowing Air to you.*
> *Deep peace of the Quiet Earth to you.*
> *Deep peace of the Shining Stars to you.*
> *Deep peace of the Son of Peace to you.*

As Ian Bradley puts it:

> *Our Celtic Christian forebears did espouse quite unashamedly and unconsciously what would nowadays be called a creation-centred spirituality. The God whom they worshipped was not conceived of primarily as the Lord of History, as in so much later Western theology, but rather as the Lord of Creation, the one who has revealed himself most fully and characteristically in the wonders and splendours of the natural world. This was above all why they wanted to worship him.*

This was far different from the pantheistic concepts of their pagan contemporaries, who worshipped the gods of rivers, mountains, winds and sun etc. It was a thoroughly Biblical understanding of God, His presence and our relationship with Him.

Plants such as the primula are indigenous to English soil and flourish easily and naturally: in the same way, the Celts are part of our spiritual DNA and the Celtic inheritance is fertile soil for the rebuilding of the nation's spiritual character. We need to take the old stones of Celtic Christianity and fashion them into paths that are relevant to today's culture.

Patriotism Without An Enemy

I mentioned earlier that we need to discover a new patriotism - without an enemy. Singer songwriter Billy Bragg has developed an interest in English national identity and in *The Progressive Patriot* expresses the view that patriotism can be reclaimed from the right wing. Bragg's notion of Englishness is not built on nostalgia, nor is it threatened by immigration, multiculturalism or Europe. He suggests that you don't have to be a red-faced retired colonel or a skinhead to love your country. Bragg says:

> *My book doesn't really belong to that genre of white middle-aged men of a certain class complaining about what it used to be like in some so-called golden age. I love my country but not in the way that Roger Scruton or Peter Hitchens do, which is based on a single idea that is stuck in the past somewhere. My England is not just the past, it's the here and now. History resonates. It's all around us and it's always there, whether I am walking up to the Roman hill fort near where I was brought up in Barking or wandering through the streets of Soho today. I can feel it now, I don't long to go back to any other time. When the St George flag is waved in Trafalgar Square when we win the Ashes, it means one thing: this is who we are. This is our team and this is what they look like. One is a Sikh, one is a Muslim.*

Bragg refers to George Orwell's essay *The Lion and the Unicorn: Socialism and the English Genius*, which John Major quoted in his now infamous anti-European Union speech in 1993, extolling the national characteristics as '*long shadows on county [cricket] grounds, warm beer, invincible green suburbs, dog lovers and pools fillers and, as George Orwell said, old maids bicycling to Holy Communion through the morning mist*'. He points out that Orwell's original vision of Englishness was, unlike Major's, extraordinarily contemporary rather than unrealistically nostalgic. Alongside the old maids on wheels, it also included *'lorries on the Great North Road'* and *'the queues outside the labour exchange'*.

The English increasingly feel impotent in expressing their patriotism, fearing it may automatically be assumed that there is right wing, racist and Europhobic baggage attached to the term. Those born before the reign of the present queen can unwittingly present a nostalgic view, characterised by all the things that have been lost: Empire, a weakened monarchy, status as a world power, breakdown of law and order, an all powerful Europe. Billy Bragg's brand of inclusive patriotism without cloying nostalgia is a large step in the right direction.

Dissenting Tradition

The English are natural dissenters. Ever since good old King Hal broke with Rome because he couldn't get his way over who he could marry, there has been a rich tradition of dissent. This has never led to revolution as on the Continent, but many of England's finest can trace their roots back to the Protestant dissenting sects of the 17th century, collectively known as the Independents. These groups were united by a belief in congregational administration of church and religious matters without any political or ecclesiastical interference; indeed, the divisions that emerged within Protestantism in the hundred years that followed the English Reformation were not founded on great theological differences, but rather on response to the imposition of authority.

This love of freedom and democracy is quintessentially English: William Blake is a superb example of a Christian believer who insisted on personal freedom from ecclesiastical authority. There is the same strain of anti-authoritarianism present in English popular and folk music, from the songs of The Kinks, The Who, Small Faces in the sixties, through Fairport Convention to The Clash and of course Billy Bragg. John Wesley was a reluctant dissenter and never formally left the Church Of England; however when banned from Anglican pulpits he preached in the open air. Had he just toed the line, thousands would not have been reached with the Gospel. This is not the spirit of rebellion, but rather an instinct to stay *within* existing structures but bend them a bit.

Billy Bragg discovered that his East London ancestors were Baptists, part of the dissenting tradition. *'I always felt instinctively that I came from the dissenting tradition,'* says Bragg, *'and then to find out that my great-great-great grandfather, George Bragg, preached in the fields and refused to sit behind the squire in church - that was a great moment.'* The healthy disregard for deference that the English rediscovered in the sixties is the flowering of a dissenting tradition which had already expressed itself in the arrival of universal suffrage, the National Health Service and the right to a free education.

Tony Benn

Tony Benn was taught to believe that the greatest sins in life were to waste time and money. His father William Wedgwood Benn was a Liberal MP who defected to Labour and was later elevated to the House of Lords with the title of 1st Viscount Stansgate. Both his grandfathers Sir John Williams Benn (who founded the family publishing house) and Daniel Holmes were also Liberal MPs. His mother Margaret (1897-1991), was a dedicated theologian, founder

President of the Congregational Federation and feminist. She was a member of the League of the Church Militant which was the predecessor of the Movement for the Ordination of Women. In 1925 she was rebuked by Randall Thomas Davidson, the then Archbishop of Canterbury, for advocating the ordination of women.

His mother's theology had a profound influence on Tony Benn, as she taught him to support the prophets and not the Kings, as the prophets taught righteousness. Benn said:

> *My mother used to read the Bible to me every night. She told me that the story of the Bible is the story of the conflict between the kings and the prophets: the kings who have power and the prophets who teach righteousness. She taught me to support the prophets over the kings. It's got me into a lot of trouble in my life! But the older I get, the more relevant I find it.*

He continues: *'I think dissent is the conscience or the spirit of the country in protest, and I think the Criminal Justice Act will be repealed in some form because you can't have a situation where a policeman can tell you where you can protest, or not.'* Benn's Socialism is rooted in dissenting ideologies as diverse as Methodism or Marx, and his links to the Labour movement run deep. On his wall is a beautiful framed Biblical allusion, given to him by his father when a boy: *'Dare to be a Daniel, Dare to stand alone, Dare to have a purpose firm, Dare to let it (be) known.'*

Mention of Tony Benn at most Christian gatherings is likely to have the ladies reaching for the smelling salts. He has the unshakeable certainty of a cult leader, with a messianic glint in his eye; his judgment can be appalling and his espousal of Arthur Scargill was surely one of his most noticeable errors of judgment. The Union leader with the stylish comb-over was clearly in politics for himself and it just happened that the Miners were a convenient cause. As with many ideologues, the cataracts of ideology can blind him to major character defects in others: Eric Heffer, veteran left-winger and close friend of Benn, was palpably a grubby and objectionable man and Benn was often forced, through shared ideology, to associate with those who didn't share his integrity, kindness and personal charm. Those who turn their back so completely on a privileged background often become its most hardened opponents.

Benn also has an almost manically naive belief in the essential goodness of human nature, a view I do not share; however, there is much the Church can learn from him, not least as a representative of that dissenting tradition which runs so deep in the English character. Careful study of his writings reveals a surprisingly sensible Socialism mingled with integrity and passion, rooted in the Bible and with a bias to the poor. The dissenting tradition is one of the building blocks of the English character and we need to find new ways of fashioning this rock into shapes that will re-establish the nation's ethical and moral foundations.

Rebuilding The Walls

The books of Ezra and Nehemiah in the Old Testament describe the building of the temple and the building of the walls, both needed for security and strength. The book of Nehemiah falls into two parts: the first six chapters cover the reconstruction of the wall, while chapters seven through to thirteen deal with the reinstruction of the people. A wall symbolizes strength and protection and in ancient cities the only real means of defence were the walls. Sometimes these walls were tremendously thick and high: the walls of the city of Babylon, as recounted in the story of Daniel, were some 380 feet thick and over 100 feet high - massive, tremendous walls.

Nehemiah remained in Judea for thirteen years as governor, carrying out many reforms, despite the opposition that he encountered (Nehemiah 13:11). He built up the State on the old lines, supplementing and completing the work of Ezra and making all arrangements for the safety and good government of the city. At the close of this important period of his public life, he returned to Persia to the service of his royal master at Shushan or Ecbatana.

Some commentators believe that Malachi now appeared among the people with words of stern reproof and solemn warning. When Nehemiah again returned from Persia - after an absence of some two years - he was grieved to see the widespread moral degeneracy that had taken place during his absence. He rebuilt the walls from the Sheep Gate in the North, the Hananel Tower at the North West corner, the Fish Gate in the West, the Furnaces Tower at the Temple Mount's South West corner, the Dung Gate in the South, the East Gate and the gate beneath the Golden Gate in the East. He set himself with vigour to rectify the flagrant abuses that had sprung up, and restored the orderly administration of public worship and the outward observance of the Law of Moses (Nehemiah 13:6-31).

There is also the need for caution. When Nehemiah comes back to Jerusalem and rides about the city he doesn't just rush out and get all the people excited to build the walls. The first thing he does is to go out at night when no one else knows, ride around the walls of the city, and survey the ruins. He takes note of exactly what needs to be done and then lays his plans.

Spraying Deodorant on the Carcass

The programme of rebuilding centred on the ten gates of the city of Jerusalem, and space only permits us to look at one of these gates - the Old Gate, mentioned in verse six. This gate symbolises God, and Truth, which will never change. It is always old, and it is upon old things that the new rests. Somebody once put it: *'Whatever is true is not new, and whatever is new is not true.'* The rebuilding of this wall is an urgent task in the life of our nation, at a time when old truths are being discarded carelessly, like unwanted clothes given to the charity shop. This erosion of the shared Christian consensus is possibly most obvious in the realm of morality, but the answer is not to buy more cans of deodorant to spray on the carcass. Since the rose has been attacked at the roots, the problem will only be solved by repairing and revitalising those roots. The answer is to rebuild the walls of truth.

There is the story of the man who one day went to visit an old musician. He knocked on the musician's door and said. *'What's the good word for today?'* The old musician didn't say a word. He turned around and went back across the room to where a tuning fork was hanging. He took a hammer and struck the tuning fork so that the note resounded through the room. Then the musician said, *'That, my friend, is 'A'. It was 'A' yesterday. It was 'A' five thousand years ago and it will be 'A' five thousand years from now.'* Then he added, *'The tenor across the hall sings off-key. The soprano upstairs is flat on her high notes. And the piano in the next room is out of tune.'* He struck the tuning fork again and said, *'That is 'A' and that, my friend, is the good word for today.'*

This is a compelling picture of the way the walls of any life, of any local church, of any community, of any nation, can be rebuilt into strength and power and purpose again.

It is clear that these spiritual and moral walls need to be rebuilt in England: exactly how is outside the scope of this book.

Persecution

I doubt if anyone in their right mind would welcome persecution. Around the world, the Christian Church is persecuted and often has to operate underground, but faith emerges stronger, purified by fire. We need a revival of faith, not religion, and if persecution is the only way that our faith in the UK can be strengthened, then so be it. Christians are sometimes too quick to adopt a 'victim' mentality, but there is evidence to suggest that Christianity is discriminated against.

In the case of the nurse who was suspended for offering to pray for a patient, I believe that she crossed the line in blurring the personal and professional boundaries and was right to be reprimanded: how would we feel if a witch offered to put a curse on someone whilst pursuing her professional duties? It is true that Christianity is having a hard time in this country at present, but we need to pick our battles and not adopt a siege mentality, huddled under the bedclothes waiting for the next wave of humanist attack.

There are a growing number of Christians who feel uncomfortable with the notion of a 'Christian Voice' in this country, especially if that voice is associated with a particularly virulent right wing agenda: bombing abortion clinics in the U.S., imposing the death penalty for gays in Uganda, racism and all manner of unpleasantness. The British National Party promises in its manifesto to '*restore Christian values to Britain*'. God help us.

Evangelical Left

Over the last fifty years or so, Christianity has begun to shed its association with anti-intellectualism, Evangelicals began graduating from college in record numbers, and Christian philanthropists began building an *'intellectual infrastructure'*. A new class of thinkers emerged representing what some have called *'the opening of the evangelical mind'*, and a solid religious left in the U.S. began to take shape, symbolized most powerfully by Barack Obama and a now twice reborn Jimmy Carter.

Until the emergence of this evangelical left, the general perception was of only one major Christian 'voice' in the marketplace: that associated with the religious right, the Southern Bible Belt in the U.S., and the oddly acultural, conservative Festival of Light/Mary Whitehouse stance in the UK; until more recently it was possible to detect an anti-intellectual bias in the newer churches in the UK. This is starting to change and a more thoughtful, reflective Christianity is emerging as the success of the Alpha course, and its offshoots, bears witness. Simon Mayo, broadcaster and now columnist for *The Times*, is a good visual aid to a less strident, gentler and culturally relevant faith.

In Britain, the Greenbelt Festival has occupied the evangelical left terrain, being prepared to push the boat out theologically, resulting in an edgy, sometimes disastrous, but always exciting event. In recent years it has become a lot smaller, but I still predict good times ahead for the Festival. In connection with Greenbelt, mention must be made of the wise, witty and infinitely kind Stewart Henderson, for many years Festival co-host and now to be found presenting arts programmes for Radio 4.

Social Entrepreneurs

A social entrepreneur is someone who recognizes a social problem and uses entrepreneurial principles to organize, create, and manage a venture to effect social change. A good current example would be Sir Peter Vardy, who took control of the car dealership Reg Vardy plc in 1976, after the death of his father. In January 2006 the dealership was sold to Pendragon, the largest UK car dealership chain, for £506m. Vardy stepped down as Chief Executive the following month.

As a committed Christian, he has been at the forefront of business involvement in education, and funded the building of a City Technology College in Gateshead and three Academies in Middlesbrough, Thorne and Blyth. These four schools form a coalition of schools with a Christian ethos based in the North of England and have received Ofsted ratings from '*good*' to '*outstanding*'. The Vardy Foundation was established in 1987 and since then has awarded grants and made donations to hundreds of worthy causes and organisations.

Less well known is Steve Holmes. He set up the Genesis Business and Enterprise Centre in Ilkeston, Derbyshire. Genesis runs a Family Entertainment Centre for the local community, including ten-pin bowling, café, sports hall and community rooms. There is also a youth work centre, a conference facility, an adult education centre and a vocational academy for 14-16 year olds. Vardy, Holmes and others are only following in a long line of Christian businessmen.

This is an area where the Church needs to encourage much greater involvement. The great Victorian social entrepreneurs like Rowntree and Cadbury were passionate, motivated individuals who understood that workers should be nurtured and cared for, provided with good facilities. Cadbury's was a business founded on strong Christian values and a sense of social responsibility. The Cadbury family believed tea, coffee and cocoa beverages could serve as an alternative to alcohol, seen to be a cause of poverty and deprivation amongst the working classes. They were involved in the early anti-slavery movement, calls for better housing and sanitation, and inner city smoke abatement.

Several of the now famous league football clubs were set up by Christian businessmen for the benefit of their employees. Over a century ago, a wealthy East End shipbuilder founded Thames Ironworks Football Team and in 1897, Arnold Hills paid for a new stadium; in 1904, under the new name of West Ham United, they moved to their present home in Upton Park. For Hills it was part of his long campaign to keep his workers away from the bottle and engage them in healthy outdoor pursuits. Like many Victorian businessmen, he had his workers' welfare at heart; he lived among them, in East India Dock Road, and would spend evenings dreaming up schemes for their education and moral well-being. A committed Christian, he encouraged all his men to 'sign the pledge', to renounce the booze that destroyed many of their lives. However, he knew that wasn't enough. He had to give them a counter-attraction to keep them out of the pubs.

Tradition of Social Care

As well as rediscovering its role in business, the Church in the UK needs to rediscover its central role as an agent of social welfare. It is clear from earlier chapters that the great, largely Christian, social movements of the 18th and 19th centuries have left their legacy; however, the church has largely subcontracted its social role to the state, so that we have *'help without the heart'* in social services.

Adrian Wooldridge, the atheist co-author of *God is Back* acknowledges:

> *Care is actually better if it is provided in a faith context. If you look at social services you have to fill in forms, people are antagonistic or they do it because they have to, whereas if you go to church for help you know you are **talking to another human being who actually cares**. These are things that religion is very good at, that bureaucratic welfare systems can't do.*

That Wooldridge is correct is substantiated by the endless succession of cases like Victoria Climbie and Baby P: care cannot be dispensed like tax advice. We see social workers being disciplined and sacked and social services chiefs announcing that *'lessons have been learned'*, when clearly they have not.

There is a great tradition of social care within the Catholic Church. Father Giovanni Bosco, or Don Bosco as he was universally known, died in Turin in 1888, but during his life he had set up hostels for the reception of those with nowhere to go, workshops and schools of arts and trades to enable them to find work and make an honest living; schools for humanities and recreational initiatives typical of his time such as drama groups, bands, choirs and youth clubs who organized away-days.

Celtic Football Club

Glasgow, one of the earliest cities of the industrial revolution, was still in the throes of its development in late Victorian times. There had been mass migration into the city - both Irish and Highland labourers had arrived by the thousand, forced by poverty to flee their land in search of better times in the city, drawn by the hope engendered by the industrial revolution. Close-packed in unhygienic slums, cholera was rife, while education and health provision were almost non-existent to those without means.

Traditional structures of education had become ineffective in this new social landscape and efforts were made by various philanthropists, educators and churchmen to meet the new needs. The Catholic Church, despite its poverty and paucity of resources was already active in social care, and priests sent to care for the people recognized education as a key weapon in the struggle against dehumanising poverty.

In 1887 Celtic Football Club was founded by Catholic educator and social reformer Walfrid, a member of the Marist Brothers, in St Mary's Church Hall in East Rose Street. He came up with the name Celtic in order to reflect his Irish and Scottish roots. His aim was to improve the social conditions of Glasgow's poverty-stricken East End – an early example of the unity of vision which has characterized the Catholic Church's understanding of these apparently separate areas of life, education, sport and social care. Celtic Football Club played its first official match on 28th May 1888, winning 5-2 against Rangers, thereby providing not simply engagement for the young, but also income to provide soup kitchens for the needy in the city.

Centre of Gravity Needs to Change

As I have already mentioned, the Church is not very good at producing individuals who are equally at home within the church and wider society. The 'centre of gravity' of many Christians is skewed: it tends to be concentrated in the Church – which is unbiblical - rather than in wider society - which is biblical. Believers should be running mainstream bookshops, mainstream record shops, mainstream law firms, mainstream sports clubs and so on. Believers need to be rooted and grounded in the local church, but living their lives in mainstream society. I use the adjective 'mainstream' rather than 'secular' (often used by Christians to denote anything non-church based), because secular implies an alternative - sacred - and I am not comfortable with the notion of a sacred/secular divide. The term 'mainstream' reinforces the idea that it is the natural place to be!

This wonky centre of gravity produces the Christian 'ghetto' of Christian music, Christian dentists, Christian books, Christian tattoo artists. Christianity is meant to be a *counter-culture*, not a sub-culture. Perhaps it comes from a misunderstanding of scripture, which needs to be corrected from the pulpit. The Church needs to take every opportunity to engage with culture, rather than avoiding it. The great Victorian philanthropists and businessmen intuitively understood their role in society and influenced millions for good: we need to rediscover this today.

True Prophets Stick Close to Scripture

The true prophet is valuable and treasured and therefore, like Rolex watches, will be counterfeited. Jesus said that many would come in His name and to some, he would say *'I never knew you'*. We are told in scripture that in the last

317

days many prophets will arise: by *'their fruits we shall know them'* and true prophets always stay close to God's written word. Christians need to pray for true prophets to emerge who can speak on national and international stages, whose hearts are breaking for the people, who can minister the compassion of Christ to a fast disintegrating world.

God has others like Bono waiting in the wings: men and women who have paid the price of obscurity and humility, whose spiritual foundations are secure and who burn with a passion and purity to see God's Kingdom come. Often, their character will have been forged through adversity. Some are already in local churches, waiting for the apostle to recognise and release them; local pastors and ministers need to look out for unusual people who don't comfortably fit the mould. These trainee prophets need to be steeped in the Word of God, happy to work in a team situation, accountable to local leaders.

The Church needs to Pray

'I fear the prayers of John Knox more than all the assembled armies of Europe.' Thus said Mary, Queen of Scots. If one looks at the history of revivals over the centuries, they have always been preceded by persistent, patient prayer, usually over many years. One of the Bible's key verses on prayer is found in the second book of Chronicles. It's phrased as a promise - a contract, if you like. God promises, if you'll do this, I'll do that: *'If my people, who are called by my name, will humble themselves and pray and seek my face and turn from their wicked ways, **then** will I hear from heaven and will forgive their sin and will heal their land.'*

'Turn from their wicked ways' sounds very heavy and conjures up the idea of idolatry, fornication, gluttony and any

number of horrid vices. However, I think it can often mean the idolatry we have in our hearts, where something other than God is enthroned. Jesus had much to say about our attitudes to wealth and possessions; 'adultery in our hearts', the things unseen by others. The Christian Church is often very severe on sexual sin, and although standards of morality are important, this type of failing is no better or worse than the others.

If a real crisis was to hit our shores, where would people instinctively go? Into the pubs? Possibly. Into the churches? I rather think so. Even though many of our churches lie dormant, there is still a network of God-fearing believers knitted together by prayer, ready to do battle for a nation which has largely said goodbye to its Christian heritage. Tom Davies again: *'the whole country is one vast web of secret prayer; there are untold thousands of secret places of prayer and if God does decide on the return of the Son of Man, a large number of people will not be taken by surprise since they are still waiting patiently and faithfully.'*

Ancient Words

As always, *'judgment starts at the House of God'* and the future of the nation is in the hands - and mouths - of believers. Although evangelistic crusades, Alpha courses and social action will always have their place, prayer is the catalyst which moves God's hand.

Words of scripture - ancient words - will appear on walls and boarded-up shops, sanctified graffiti. Old Bibles which have remained on shelves for years and years will be dusted down and read. The English will rediscover ancient words, stored in their subconscious and handed down by past generations, and be delighted and revitalised by their surprising familiarity. Let us remind ourselves what R. S. Thomas, in his *The Country Clergy*, said:

> *Venerable men, their black cloth a little dusty*
> *They left no books*
> *Memorial to their lonely thought*
> *In grey parishes; rather they wrote*
> *On men's hearts and in the minds of young children*
> *Sublime words too soon forgotten.*
> *God in his time*
> *Or out of time will correct this.*

Revivals

The Welsh Revival of 1904-05 was a divine intervention that drastically changed lives in churches, homes, mines, factories, schools and places of leisure and entertainment. Prayer meetings for world revival were being held in many places throughout the nation. Evan Roberts, the man most associated with the Revival, spent seven hours in prayer and Bible study each day.

Sustained prayer must be the norm if we are to experience the birth pangs of a new spiritual era. Roberts received an overwhelming 'burden' for the soul of his nation. He began asking God for 100,000 people to be converted and he spent nights in prayer. He was the principal character that God used to birth the Welsh Revival. '*You must put yourself entirely at the Holy Spirit's disposal*' he once said.

John and Charles Wesley and George Whitefield were present at the beginning of the Evangelical Revival. '*It was a Pentecostal season indeed,*' said Whitefield, '*Sometimes whole nights were spent in prayer. Often we have been filled as with new wine!*'

The Hebridean revival of 1949-1953 started with two old women praying together. Duncan Campbell, who was the main preacher there during this period writes:

> *In the parish of Barvas a number of men and women took a call to prayer to heart, especially two old women. I am ashamed to think of it - two sisters, one eighty-two and one eighty-four, the latter blind. These two women developed a great heart concern for God to do something in the parish and gave themselves to waiting upon God in their little cottage. Sending for the minister, one of the sisters told him their story, and he took her message as a word from God to his heart. Turning to her he said, 'What do you think we should do?'' She said, 'Give yourself to prayer; give yourself to waiting upon God. Get your elders and deacons together and spend at least two nights a week waiting upon God in prayer. If you will do that at your end of the parish, my sister and I will do it at our end of the parish from ten o'clock at night until two or three o'clock in the morning.'*

The Last Word

As we draw to a close, I hope some of the topics touched upon in this final chapter resonate with you. The last word, however, goes to Korean David Yonggi Cho, Senior Pastor and founder of the Yoido Full Gospel Church (Assemblies of God), the world's largest congregation with a membership of 830,000. Cho still conducts two out of the seven services the church holds every day; they are so heavily attended that people often must arrive an hour early to secure a seat. Raised initially as a Buddhist, Cho converted to Christianity at the age of 19, after an unknown girl visited him daily telling him abou tthe love of Christ, after he was diagnosed with terminal tuberculosis. One day, she knelt down to pray for him and began to weep. He was deeply touched and told her, *'Don't cry... I now know about your Christian love. Since I am dying I will become a Christian for you.'*

There is a persistent anecdote that has been heard several times at Church conferences: the story is that Cho was a guest on one of the big U.S. talk-shows - Jay Leno or David Letterman or someone like that. The interview went like this:

Interviewer:
You have the world's biggest church. How did you do it?

Cho:
We pray.

Interviewer:
I see. Now, what is your strategy?

Cho:
Ah ... We pray.

Interviewer:
OK, let me ask this a different way. What are the distinctive things about your church that mark it out as different from others, and that have contributed to your success?

Cho:
We pray.

Epilogue

England! awake! awake! awake!
Jerusalem thy sister calls!
Why wilt thou sleep the sleep of death
And close her from thy ancient walls?
Thy hills and valleys felt her feet
Gently upon their bosoms move:
Thy gates beheld sweet Zion's ways;
Then was a time of joy and love.
And now the time returns again:
Our souls exult, and London's towers
Receive the Lamb of God to dwell
In England's green and pleasant bowers.

William Blake
Jerusalem

BIBLIOGRAPHY

Ackroyd, Peter: *Albion: the Origins of the English Imagination*
Ackroyd, Peter: *Blake*
Ackroyd, Peter: *London - The Biography*
Azariah, V. S, Bishop: *In the Shadow of the Mahatma*
Babatunde, Wale: *Great Britain has Fallen*!
Barr, Charles: *Ealing Studios*
Bell, Stuart: *Rebuilding the Walls*
Benn, Tony: *Free At Last!*
Bentley Jr, G. E: *The Stranger from Paradise - a Biography of William Blake*
Bjorklund, David F: *Why Youth Is Not Wasted on the Young*
Bragg, Billy: *The Progressive Patriot*
Brierley, Peter: *'Christian' England*
Brown, Calum: *The Death of Christian Britain*
Calhoun, Scott: *@U2.com website*
Cannadine, David: *In Churchill's Shadow*
Carey, S. Pearce: *William Carey*
Cheetham, J. K: *On the Trail of John Wesley*
Clatworthy, Jonathan: *Liberal Faith in a Divided Church*
Colls, Robert: *Identity of England*
Davies, Tom: *Merlyn the Magician and the Pacific Coast Highway*
Davies, Tom: *Testament*
Davies, Tom: *The Man of Lawlessness*
Dimbleby, Jonathan: *The Prince of Wales*
Dixon, Patrick: *Futurewise*
Fendall, Lon: *William Wilberforce*
Fitzgerald, F. Scott: *The Great Gatsby*
Fitzgerald, F. Scott: *Tender is the Night*
Fox, Kate: *Watching the English*
Gandhi, M. K: *An Autobiography*
Geldof, Bob: *Is that it?*

Green, Roger. J: *William Booth*
Hague, William: *William Wilberforce*
Hattersley, Roy: *A Brand from the Burning: John Wesley*
Hattersley, Roy: *Borrowed Time*
Hattersley, Roy: *The Edwardians*
Hennessy, Peter: *Having it so Good - Britain in the Fifties*
Hill, Clifford: *The Wilberforce Connection*
Himmelfarb, Gertrude: *Poverty and Compassion*
Hoare, Philip: *Noel Coward*
James, Lawrence: *Raj: The Making & Unmaking of British India*
Jenkins, Roy: *Churchill*
Jenkins, Roy: *Gladstone*
Junor, Penny: *The Firm: The Troubled Life of the House of Windsor*
Kimbrough, S. T: *Charles Wesley - Poet and Theologian*
Kingsnorth, Paul: *Real England*
Koch, Richard & Smith, Chris: *Suicide of the West*
Mandleson, Peter: *The Third Man*
Letts, Quentin: *Fifty People Who Buggered Up Britain*
Mandler, Peter: *The English National Character*
Mangalwadi, Vishal: *William Carey*
Marr, Andrew: *A History of Modern Britain*
McCulloch, Diarmaid: *The History of Christianity*
Micklethwait, John & Wooldridge, Adrian: *God is Back*
Morgan, Kenneth O: *Britain Since 1945 - The People's Peace*
Neuberger, Julia: *The Moral State We are in*
Nicolson, Juliet: *The Perfect Summer - Dancing into Shadow in 1911*
Noble, John: *The Shaking*
Paxman, Jeremy: *On Royalty*
Paxman, Jeremy: *The English - Portrait of a People*
Peston, Robert: *Who Runs Britain?*
Picard, Liza: *Victorian London*
Saunders, Andrew: *Charles Dickens*
Shannon, Richard T: *Gladstone: God and Politics*

Stanford, Peter: *The Outcast's Outcast - A Biography of Lord Longford*

Starkey, Mike: *Frogs & Princes*

Stedman, Ray C: *Nehemiah: Rebuilding the Wall*

Steer, Roger: *George Muller*

Stephens, Philip: *Tony Blair*

Tabraham, Barrie W: *Brother Charles*

Thwaites, James: *The Church Beyond the Congregation*

Tomalin, Claire: *Thomas Hardy*

Turner, Alwyn W: *Crisis? What Crisis?*

Turner, John Munsey: *John Wesley*

Wakelin, Michael: *J. Arthur Rank*

Waller, Ralph: *John Wesley*

Wallis, Jim: *God's Politics*

Weintraub, Stanley: *Albert*

Wilson, A .N: *Our Times*

Wilson, A. N: *After the Victorians*

Wilson, A. N: *God's Funeral*

Wilson, A. N: *The Victorians*

Windsor, Duke of: *A King's Story*